*The spirit of a man will [sustain him]
but a wounded sp[irit who can bear?]*

*- Prover[bs 18:14]*

# BIBLICAL CURES FOR THE WOUNDED SPIRIT

*Answers for PTSD and Healing the invisible Wound*

## WAYNE A. KEAST

ARPress

Copyright © 2024 by Wayne A. Keast

All rights reserved. No part of this publication may be reproduced, distributed, or transmitted in any form or by any means, including, photocopying,recording, or other electronic or mechanical methods, without the prior written permission of the copyright owner and the publisher, except in the case of brief quotations embodied in critical reviews and certain other noncommercial uses permitted by copyright law. For permission requests, write to the publisher, addressed "Attention: Permissions Coordinator," at the address below.

**ARPress**
45 Dan Road Suite 5
Canton MA 02021
Hotline: 1(888) 821-0229
Fax: 1(508) 545-7580

Ordering Information:
Quantity sales. Special discounts are available on quantity purchases by corporations, associations, and others. For details, contact the publisher at the address above.

Printed in the United States of America.

| ISBN-13: | Softcover | 979-8-89389-527-8 |
|---|---|---|
| | eBook | 979-8-89389-528-5 |

Library of Congress Control Number: 2024920134

# Table of Contents

Dedication page .................................................................................. I

Foreword....................................................................................... III

Abbreviations .............................................................................. VII

## Part I

Chapter 1 : Introduction .......................................................................1

Chapter 2 : Background ........................................................................7

Chapter 3 : "Advancements" ................................................................15

Chapter 4 : Various Worldviews ..........................................................22

Chapter 5 : The Importance of the Mind ...........................................33

Chapter 6 : Various Aspects of Remedies for PTSD.............................47

Chapter 7 : Which brings us to today..................................................57

Chapter 8 : Is Today's Psychology the Best Way? .................................71

## Part II

Chapter 9 : Fear (Anxiety)...................................................................98

Chapter 10 : Guilt, theoretical ..........................................................110

Chapter 11 : Nightmares and Flashbacks, theoretical ........................123

Chapter 12 : Anger, theoretical..........................................................134

Chapter 13 : Isolation or Avoidance, theoretical ...............................141

Chapter 14 : Pain and Suffering, theoretical .....................................147

Conclusion........................................................................................152

Epilogue............................................................................................157

Appendix..........................................................................................158

Biblical Meditation ............................................................................158

Glossary ...............................................................................161

Selected Bibliography ........................................................................164

Periodicals ..........................................................................................178

Electronic Documents ........................................................................179

# Dedication Page

To God be the glory, great things He hath done. Amidst, and regardless the turmoil of deployments, surgeries and uncertainties of military life, God's unseen hand was upon my career and guided me to new adventures and ministries. This book is dedicated to Jesus Christ, those chaplains, physicians who have made a difference to our troops in the various war zones, and to those who have served in our Armed Forces in peace and in war: In the past and presently. To particularly those who have given their lives and to those who have been physically and spiritually wounded.

# Foreword

## The reason for writing this book

I write this book, *Bible Cures for the Wounded Spirit: PTSD and Healing the Invisible Wound* to develop in the reader an understanding for the importance of the true nature of PTSD, what it brings to its victim and through the historical background what brings the ultimate cure a rich faith in Jesus Christ that comes through the Scripture. Also, my intent is to make aware to all who contend with PTSD, whether personally or someone near them, that a personal faith in Jesus Christ and all the emotional support He can provide is, unlike popular drug treatment, psychological therapy, or New Age philosophies applications are without side effects. Within these pages I attempt to explain what I see through history and Scriptures what brings PTSD about. Due to the amount of false hope given through the plethora of supposed cures, I also give reasons why counterfeits do not work and are even dangerous.

If someone reading this book has never asked Jesus Christ to be their personal Savior, to forgive them of their sins, to be saved by trusting alone in the shed blood of Jesus Christ that He shed on the cross for them, I invite you to stop reading this, bow your head, and based on Romans 10:9 (That if thou shalt confess with thy mouth the Lord Jesus, and shalt believe in thine heart that God hath raised him from the dead, thou shalt be saved), receive Christ right now. If you prayed, asking Jesus to save you, then you have God living inside of you, and that step of faith is this first crucial step in letting God minister to you and solving your PTSD. Growth in Jesus Christ is the key resource to overcoming PTSD. All experiences one has endured to bring about PTSD in their life, those experiences while not be erased. However, the experiences can be replaced through the Word of God, the Bible. A consistent, faithful exposure to the Bible, individually and corporately through doses of scripture preaching at church services will in time bring victory over Post Traumatic Stress.

This book is an added resource to help victims cope with PTSD symptoms. Finding the root causes of PTSD and to overcome the associated issues that draw from PTSD are also addressed. I believe that improvements can be made in therapy by implementing biblical teaching in place of much of what are current answers that have been suggested by the psychological and medical communities. These communities, though they mean well, are not equipped to treat the soul, which ought to be the target and the key issue. Scripture treats the soul. The current treatment shortcomings are demonstrated via two avenues: confronting the PTSD sufferer with their personal experiences of increased stress levels, and the lack of progress they experience through other means. In addition, the possible dangers that may arise as will be described below. Also examined are the differences between this program, based on biblical promises, and the current treatment modalities. Jesus Christ, as your Savior, walking by your side, living in you, is your go-to battle buddy in resolving PTSD issues.

If you have just prayed to receive Jesus Christ as your Savior, please contact me at woundedspiritsministry@gmail.com. We would love to celebrate with you and to help further with other valuable resources.

# Abbreviations

*DSM*
Diagnostic and Statistical Manual of Mental Disorders 5th Edition DSM-5
*KJV*  King James Version
*PTSD*  Post-Traumatic Stress Disorder
*TBI*  Traumatic brain injury
*WTB*  Warrior Transition Battalion

# Part I

# CHAPTER 1

## Introduction

**Background**

"Twenty-two veterans commit suicide every day."[1] This statement reflects an American tragedy. Secretary of Defense Leon Panetta testified before the House Armed Services and Veterans Affairs committees in 2012 about the veterans' suicide rate.

The issue preying on him was not the defeat of the Taliban or extermination of al-Qaeda, much less contingency planning for feared budget cuts. No, the issue Panetta had in mind and labeled a top priority was the runaway suicide rate in the military, averaging thirty-three suicides per month in 2012, roughly one every seventeen hours.[2]

What, however, is not mentioned are the statistics coming from the states to the federal agencies that

---
1   Stacy Bare, "The Truth About 22 Veterans Suicides a Day, accessed July 20, 2017. http://taskandpurpose.com.
2   Robert Emmet Meager, *Killing from the Inside Out: Moral injury and Just War* (Eugene, OR: Cascade Books), 211–217. Kindle.

report their numbers. Only twenty-one states report statistics. Not reported in the article is that twenty-nine states do not disclose information concerning their suicides. Two million, six hundred thousand military members have deployed to Iraq and Afghanistan since September 11, 2001. Seven hundred thousand have gone more than once.[3]

The desire for writing this book concerns prevention or relief of Post-Traumatic Stress Disorder (PTSD), traumatic brain injury (TBI), and moral injury and how they affect US military members. I returned from Iraq in Oct 2006 serving in Iraq as a US Army chaplain. Having experienced some intense situations, my faith in God was challenged and then strengthened by meditating in and gaining an understanding of the Christian Scriptures. Many soldiers who have seen and experienced horrific events in war are returning home with emotional issues that they do not understand. Many asked questions they had never asked before and tried to subdue emotions they had never experienced. Though the military system supplied the traumatized soldier with psychology and medications, I discovered later through one-on-one personal interviews that these therapies were ultimately detrimental. Soldiers, often, not knowing where to turn, used the medications given by a physician and sometimes self-medicated adding an often-deadly alcohol mixture. They had not been exposed to the answers could be found in the Bible.

In 2008, a year after returning from Iraq deployment, God worked in me some amazing

---

3     1900 Fort Bragg soldiers to deploy this summer, Fayobserver.com, April 27, 2017.

circumstances. I had aortic valve replacement open-heart surgery, I was then assigned to a unit designed for soldiers with long-term healthcare needs, at that time known as Warrior Transition Battalion (WTB), now Soldier Recovery Unit (SRU). After assigned for rehabilitation the commander, who was short a unit chaplain, ask me to help soldiers with spiritual needs and counseling. During this time, I found through counseling conversations with soldiers that doctors or psychologists were not adequately addressing many of their emotional and spiritual problems.

As I said, many soldiers were self-medicating with alcohol. Drug addictions were epidemic, and the writing of prescriptions for soldiers struggling with PTSD was standard procedure for the doctors. God impressed upon me the need to do a Bible-level study concerning this problem that results from PTSD. I found in the Bible God's answers to PTSD and related emotional issues.

The United States Armed Forces story is one of courage, heroism, bravery, and sacrifice. It is also often an untold story; a history of traumatic experiences that often go with war and causes participants of combat to re-experience emotionally harsh events in its aftermath. These experiences of trauma are locked into the memory and emotions and affect the soul and spirit, and can reoccur through triggers. These triggers are sights, sounds, and smells, and etc. that were experienced and associated with experienced trauma. These traumas are often manifesting in what psychology and the mental health community, since the 1980's call PTSD and moral injury. By the way, it may take years for PTSD problem to come to the light. The military's medical and mental health system generally look for manifestation to occur within three months, but realistically they can occur anytime based on triggers.

United States military service members have experienced various traumas that have inspired various attempts by those in the medical, mental health, and religious communities to help find answers to these issues. These attempts have brought on rather extensive and even lengthy discourses concerning the reason for and against the plethora of resources that perhaps should not be used. This book attempts to exam the help available and what has worked best.

Highly trained warriors, prepared for battle with weapons and tactics and taught to kill, lack in one crucial area; they are not trained in how to handle killing. That is, the mental (soulish) trauma placed on a soldier taking a life or how to witness death. Death, though happening on a near-daily basis in the active war zone, is viewed as unnatural. From the beginning, God did not intend for man to die. Death came when man disobeyed God in the garden of Eden in the book of Genesis (Gen 2:17). Coupling that with the commandment "Thou shalt not kill" (Exo 20:13). There is within man's innate knowledge that killing is not right. When man committed the first sin, he immediately died in his spirit by losing his fellowship and communication with God. Satan's subtilty deceived Eve, and she ate of the forbidden fruit. Steve Curington, former drug addict and founder of Reformers Unanimous, a faith-based addiction recovery ministry, noted, "He attacked Eve's ability to trust God for what was right for her and her husband. He twisted the truth by, 'If you eat of this tree, you will be just like him.'" This began the downward spiral of death as this one act spiritually separated humanity from God. Much of the mystery of death could be resolved with decreasing stress levels with just some biblical instruction. There is power in having information, if that information is applied to self. Sadly, the current spiritual condition of America and those in charge of running the various systems within the military complex do not have regard for biblical Christianity and its key biblical philosophy concerning PTSD and moral injury recovery.

Some in our deployed military suffer from physical wounds, while those and others can suffer from a wounded spirit but were not made aware during training that such an injury is even a possibility. Though PTSD can and is often referred to as an injury of combat, it can also be a result of an assault, child abuse, natural disaster, or an accident. Some attempt to go through basic training, and while experiencing the bayonet course or rifle qualifications, sense in their spirit that the military is really about killing the enemy. Many leave the service during basic training due to "the inability to adapt." Having been a chaplain at a basic training unit, I have seen trainees experience that stress. Memories from youth can produce trauma. As a psychologist once said, "With the help of the analyst as another self who participates in the experience of affects, unincorporated effects are now made conscious and bound in the meaning that emerges from the experienced intersubjectivity in the life context of the subjects here and now."[4] While there is a broader civilian application, this book's concentration shall remain on those who received a wounded spirit in the context of violence in a war scenario, the various means by which the military attempts to bring healing, and finally what processes and materials really makes the difference in PTSD recovery.

The significance and frequency of the problem of suicide and the other issues that proceed from PTSD should be addressed. To that end, it is suggested that a person, if they have not done so, come to a personal relationship in Jesus Christ so that the Holy Spirit may begin making a new person in Christ in the individual. By doing so the relationship that has been severed by Adam as passed on to all mankind is restored through Jesus Christ and blindness experienced by man is removed and man is then capable of receiving spiritual sight, thus instruction from God. Paul explains this in Ephesians, saying, "And that ye put on the new man, which after God is created in righteousness and true holiness (Eph. 4:24). This is a crucial first decision to make in recovery. Those who feel they can see recovery without taking that step of salvation in Christ will try and ultimately fail. A relationship with Christ is seen as important throughout the studies. When one comes to Christ for salvation and a daily walk with Him begins, the issues of suicide and other issues can be targeted, and God will heal. Purpose and meaning with forgiveness and love enters one's life. Providing biblical answers is the focus here.

---

4    Angelica Rauch, Post Trauma Hermeneutic: Melancholia in the Wake of Trauma, Vol. 28, no.4 (Winter 1998).

# Chapter 2

## Background

Author Elahe Hessamfor explains his view concerning reasons or blames for various issues:

> At one point in history strange and mysterious experiences, behaviors, and ways of talking about the world were considered gifts from the gods, leading to respect, reverence and awe. At another point such experiences were assumed to be the product of demons, leading to exorcism. Later the cause of such experiences came to be located in such things as poor parenting, pathological families, sexual abuse, and difficult social conditions, thus moving the mystery outwards into the family and community. Nowadays we are taught that we should interpret unusual experiences in terms of biology, neurology, and genetics, turning the locus of interest inwards towards the individual. So, we are constantly

> shifting the causes and outcomes of mental illness upwards, outwards, inwards.[5]

Ideas have changed and will continue to over time with each discovery. God's Word does not change. It is correct from the start. The above statement is one of many examples showing the heathenistic approach that is much of psychology. The plethora of theories that continue to spew from of so many in the psychology field is frightening and evident of the continue unsolved issues of "mental illness" we are faced with today.

## PTSD: A Historical View

Finding the cause to ailments is an ongoing issue. Even so, the history of today's PTSD label gives an interesting story of the thoughts that the medical community and the psychiatric community have had in examining this problem. In fact, the terms for PTSD go beyond the boundaries of America and of any present timeframe. PTSD expert and author Chris Adsit explains:

> During the latter half of the 1600s, the Swiss observed a consistent set of symptoms in some of their soldiers and called it *nostalgia*. German doctors of the same period used the term *heimveh*, and the French called it *maladie du pays*. These terms are roughly translated as 'homesickness.'"[6]

---

5 Elahe Hessamfar, *In the Fellowship of His Suffering: A Theological Interpretation of Mental Illness* (Eugene, OR: Cascade Books, 2014), 51–55, Kindle.

6 *Chris Adsit, Combat Trauma Healing Manual (Newport News, VA: Military Ministry Press, 2007), 22.*

After the American Civil War, soldiers returning from the battles manifested problems that the newly forming psychological community was attempting to answer. Doctors would prescribe time in an insane asylum for observation and therapy. "The major threats to one's health were seen as coming from a depletion of resources that allowed powerful external stimuli to derange the system often by means of the reflex action of the nerves. Lack of sleep and proper nutrition could render a person vulnerable."[7]

It was around this time in history, the seventeenth century in Europe, Sigmund Freud began developing his theories in psychoanalysis. The Higher Criticisms of the liberal church developed, bringing with it a lessened dependence on the Christian Scriptures. Charles Darwin's *Origin of the Species* was being written and would soon become popular. All these philosophies that promoted self-help and decreased a need for God stirred mankind into believing that he was capable of managing his world alone. Dependence toward God and the Bible was decreasing.

In Europe, the doctors there during the First World War were studying their patients who had suffered from the American trauma entitled *shell shock,* calling it a "war neurosis." It had similar effects upon the individual and was characterized by "stupor, confusion, mutism, loss of sight or hearing, spasmodic convulsions or trembling of the limbs, anesthesia, exhaustion, sleeplessness, depression, and … nightmares."[8] It was

---

7   Eric T. Dean, Jr., *Shook Over Hell: Post Traumatic Stress, Vietnam and the Civil War* (Cambridge: Harvard, 1997), 146.

8   Dean, 169.

thought the victim was unable to express his experiences by describing them, so he would display symptoms. With the loss of memory, the mind would shut down, being overwhelmed and overloaded with emotions. With extreme overload came dissociation or amnesia.

The American medical and mental health communities have, in the past, attempted to diagnose with authority those with PTSD that they might receive the best care available. Stories have been documented showing the best efforts from knowledgeable doctors to be at times lacking and at worst nonexistent. In America, with psychology in its infancy, cases were documented, such as:

In January 1884, Cameron was committed to the asylum with acute mania and released about one month later as 'cured.' In May of 1884, he was readmitted with recurrent mania, held for about six months, and released again as cured. Then four years later, in late 1888, he was readmitted a third time, held for about five months, and released yet again as cured.[9]

Many similar cases are documented and move along the same refrain. Later, the information will be examined describing these kinds of medical procedures that are still in the developmental and experimental stages, and proof of their effectiveness still lacks. Medical and mental health facilities are still searching for and researching remedies.

The health department that existed in Indiana at the of time of the Civil War documented cases concerning the use of various kinds of pharmaceuticals in which

---

9   Dean, 141.

when an Indiana soldier began using narcotics, "the 22.4 percent ... of veterans in the Indiana Sample who abused alcohol, another 5.2 percent ... abused drugs, usually chloral hydrate, cocaine, morphine, or opium."[10] The symptoms of PTSD, "sleepless and disturbed by memories of the war, some veterans simply left home and went off 'tramping.'"[11]

So, what is PTSD? A military pamphlet explains, "PTSD is an emotional and behavioral disturbance that may occur after exposure to an exceptionally stressful, threatening or catastrophic event."[12] Soldiers have mental scars that may heal slowly if at all, and for some, the trauma never ends. Author Bridgett Cantrell explains that scars can come in the form of "depression, cynicism ... anger, alienation, isolation, sleep disturbances, poor concentration, tendency to react under stress with survival tactics, psychic or emotional numbing."[13] According to doctors these are just a few of the over 200 manifestations brought on by war.

Symptoms of PTSD include:

a. insomnia b. fear c. hypersensitivity to light and sound d. anxiety e. difficulty eating f. panic and paranoia g. psychosis h. seizures i. mania j. visual hallucination k. inability to function or work l. a loss of

---

10  *Ibid., 169.*
11  Ibid., 168.
12  Quick Series, Post Traumatic Stress Disorder (Canada: Quick Series Publishing, 2010).
13  Bridgett C. Cantrell and Chuck Dean, *Down Range to Iraq and Back* (Seattle: Wordsmith, 2005), 37.

sense of identity m. psychotic depression n. elevated mood and grandiose delusions o. unrestrained behaviors (sexual and violent) p. pain q confusion and disorientation r. feeling of emptiness and ennui (listlessness and dissatisfaction) s. depersonalization t. impairment of social relationships u. cognitive, perceptual and sensory aberrations v. disempowering w. causes passiveness and compliance (even when those are negative responses to certain situations). It is interesting to note that most of these symptoms that occur are similar to symptoms that occur with the use of hallucinogenic drugs.[14]

Author Serene Jones cites, "traumatic events [are ones] in which one experiences the threat of annihilation. One's continued existence is called into question by the specter of impending death or looming destruction."[15] This experience of perceived certain doom can be personal, and it can be felt for another where a similar experience is being witnessed. Jones continues, "Violent events can befall both individuals and communities, both villages and nations, both single families and whole regions."[16] To be clear, one does not need to be a warrior to experience these issues. As mentioned, the above trauma or crisis experiences of any kind can bring on PTSD. Everyone experiences crises differently. The same incident or stressor can

---

14  LT Editors, 15.
15  Serene Jones, *Trauma and Grace* (Louisville, KY: Westminster John Knox, 2009), 13.
16  Ibid., 14.

affect one far differently than it may affect another. One's temperament may be able to handle an event and not see something as traumatic while another will be traumatized by that same situation. Counselor and author Norman Wright points out, "Crises are not always bad. Rather, they represent a pivotal point in a person's life. Therefore, it can bring an opportunity as well as danger."[17]

Soldiers train to do battle with the enemy, regardless of conditions, terrain, or weather. Soldiers train to kill, but what may be the more difficult thing for some is to not know when they will be called upon to do so. Military strategist Dave Grossman declares, "There are many burdens that weigh upon the warrior, and one of the greatest is uncertainty … this toxic event can happen at any time."[18] This uncertainty removes the element of control; people, particularly warriors in combat, like to have control of the battle situation. Strategists do extensive planning to remove doubt as to an outcome of a conflict. The moment the enemy takes the initiative to begin a conflict, then the other side is in reaction mode and has lost control. To the soldier, taking the initiative means maintaining control. Keeping the initiative helps keep the element of control on their side, reducing some levels of stress. Grossman further states, "The constant anticipation of being attacked can have a profound toxic effect, especially when this high state of alert and stress continues over months and years. For the police officer or soldier,

17  H. Norman Wright, *Crisis and Trauma Counseling* (Ventura: Regal, 2003), 131.
18  Dave Grossman, *On Combat* (Washington, DC: Warrior Science Publication, 2004), 273.

there is a constant possibility that just around the next corner, there might be an individual who will dedicate all … toward snuffing your life out."[19] This is the height of trauma. Being in reaction mode is exhausting work. We see this today in our Covid-19–impacted society. The constantly daily reminders of the unseen virus will take its toll. Suicides are up, among other illnesses and societal stressors. Now, we are hearing that much of the warnings that were issued by the "experts" concerning the possible attempts at avoiding the threatened illness is has been misdiagnosed. Some claim that the attempts at lessening the consequences of the virus has actually made things worse. Yes, there are many stressors at the door, but Christ is available to be the healer.

---

19   Grossman, 273.

# Chapter 3

## "Advancements"

X-rays, scans, blood work, and other standard testing is the general rule for diagnosing injury or illness. Not so for PTSD. A clinic doctor relates:

> If someone shows up in my practice and they say that a psychiatrist or other doctor diagnosed me with PTSD, I would ask the patient, "OK, what tests were done to establish that diagnosis?" and they would think about it, and they would realize that nothing was done. They just got an opinion of whoever the practitioner was."[20]

PTSD cannot be discovered through tests; however, it was proclaimed as such by the American Psychiatric Association (APA). "It wasn't found through scientific testing, it was lobbied for by psychiatrists and voted into psychiatry's *Diagnostic and Statistical Manual*—literally voted in."[21] When psychiatrists prescribe medicines, they are done without any testing to verify

---

20  Citizens Commission on Human Rights, "The Hidden Enemy: Inside Psychiatry's Covert Agenda," (DVD), 2013.
21  Citizens Commission on Human Rights, 2013.

its effectiveness. When two or more drugs are prescribed together it is called "polypharmacy." It has been noted by one physician that, "Many of these drugs have never been tested in combination."[22]

Dr Jonathan Shay cannot wholeheartedly recommend workaholism to a person living with PTSD. He states, "After World War I and again after World War II, the German government's approach to post-combat adjustment to civilian life was work, nothing in the way of treatment for combat trauma, but a great deal in the way of vocational training, job placement."[23] Further, Shay goes on to say, "Workaholism is a very successful strategy for keeping a lid on things, for those whose luck and makeup permits it to function reliably."[24] Yet, with this seeming endorsement, Shay finally says that the German philosophy, in this case, it appears wrong.

A history of where these current-day practices originated, it was discovered how they came about, thus exposing their dangers. "[*In*] one 1950's psycho-physiology text book … it says that the function of the midbrain can be thought of as … fight, flight, feeding and mating."[25] Many soldiers and spouses have recognized the change in these areas when they return from battle.

**Bible Cure**

Even as a doctor sets a bone and the healing process begins, the Bible can set the soul for the spiritual healing

---
22   CCHR, 2013.
23   Shay, *Odysseus in America*, 59.
24   Ibid., 59.
25   Grossman, 275.

process to begin as the knowledgeable counselor gives instruction. When Jesus's disciples sought someone to take the blame for the blindness of the man born in that condition, He said the man was healed by Jesus for God's glory, not for someone to be found at fault (See John 9:1-7). The late apologist Ravi Zacharias explains, "There is no way to understand blindness of the soul until you are humble enough to know that only God can bring healing."[26] The mental health industry lacks this spiritual insight.

When lives are on the line, and if a soldier realizes that God has complete control of any situation and he need not be surprised by outcome of events and that God cannot be surprised by anything, that soldier can say with full assurance as King David did, "The angel of the LORD encampeth around about them that fear him, and delivereth them" (Psa. 34:7). That assurance comes from realizing that delivering them may mean death but also means he or she is heaven bound. Charles Stanley states, "Whether it is in our job, finances, families, or health, whatever it may be, has to happen in the presence of our loving heavenly Father. He has allowed it."[27]

The Bible passage in 1 Kings 18:21—19:8 relates where Elijah expends much energy to the point of exhaustion, defeating and killing 450 prophets of Baal and 400 grove prophets. When Queen Jezebel hears that God's prophet had killed *her* prophets, she gave Elijah twenty-four hours to live. He, in his exhaustion, ran for

---

26 Ravi Zacharias, *Beyond Opinion: Living the Faith We Defend* (Nashville, TN: Thomas Nelson, 2007), 207.
27 Charles Stanley, *God Is in Control.* Kindle, 62.

his life. He forgot God, thinking only of himself and ran into the wilderness. There, God came to his aid and allowed him to eat and sleep, with a time to refocus on God before giving him another mission. The military might do well to take this advice when it comes to the refitting and resetting the soldier and their units of assignment. Soldiers are given leave, but I dare say many soldiers give that time over to consumption of alcohol, other narcotics, and other unhealthy activities. Precious spiritual matters are rarely considered.

**Give Up Control**

When a soldier has the Christian hope within him that is durable and can overcome any trauma or stress that life can thrust on him, then that soldier has, not by his own doing or in his strength, but through God who gives the enablement to overcome PTSD every day. When God's strength comes, it will manifest as peace. God over and over tells the one who reads the Bible that peace is available to those who look to him, such as when He says, "and the peace of God, which passeth all understanding, shall keep your hearts and minds through Christ Jesus" (Phil. 4:13). Peace is foundational to living a productive life, and God promises peace to those who want it. "True peace protects. It will guard the way we think and safeguard our feeling."[28] Granted, victory over PTSD is not a once-and-done situation. It is an ongoing process, and it is an ongoing ordeal that must be defeated each time it presents itself. An individual cannot erase PTSD; the power of God replaces the traumatic episode at

---
28   Grossman, 196.

the moment when the person with PTSD decides to allow God to take control of his/her encounter with trauma or when memories persist. The mind is a critical component of fighting and winning the war on PTSD. This must include having the mind of Christ (1 Cor. 2:16; Rom. 12:2). The battle is won by the renewing in the spirit of your mind (Eph 4:23), not the brain as commonly thought.

When the individual's desires and perceived needs do not get supplied and longings go unfulfilled, some may question, where is God? God is sovereign. He is also good. God is all-wise and will not allow his children to be beggars. "He can do anything. Not only that, he claims to love us. So why does he seem to abandon us to loss, loneliness, and disappointment?"[29] It is a matter of trust. Peace comes when one is firm in the knowledge that God knows what the end will look like before the beginning and that He knows the way through any wilderness that His child may have to travel. The wilderness may include infertility or an abundant posterity, sudden illness and death of a spouse or a couple living to be one hundred. Whatever God has in mind for His children (the short, hard life or years of seeming comfort and ease), God knows best, and His plan for all is perfect and is a matter of getting self out of the way and allowing God to work His perfect plan. The challenge is to give up control.

Grossman reminds the reader, "Ultimately the limitations of our bodies and our minds determines the nature of our weapons. Of these two, the mind is by far

---

29 Dan B. Allender and Tremper Longman III, *The Cry of the Soul* (Colorado Springs: Navpress, 1994), 118, Kindle.

the most important."[30] When God comes to the soldier and puts His mind into his and gives hope and a peace that passes understanding (Phil. 4:7), the mind will be able to vanquish any fear that can be experienced because God is able to overcome any fear. Schiraldi asserts, "Life doesn't prepare us for trauma. Following exposure to traumatic events, millions of people develop PTSD or lesser forms of this condition with symptoms ranging from nightmares to headaches."[31] Life can be filled with trauma, but it is each person's choice as to how they will handle it. So, since people have a choice, why do so many choose wrong? The Bible discovers and gives the answers to this question. The prophet declared, "The heart is deceitful above all things, and desperately wicked: who can know it?" (Jer. 17:9). When Jeremiah tells the people of God that they are blessed if they choose God, he suddenly realizes the horrible condition they are in. Biblical scholar Charles L. Feinberg relates: "Jeremiah is quickly brought back to 'reality,' confronted with the depravity of human nature, a depravity that is about to cost thousands of people their lives under the crushing weight of the covenantal curses for disobedience ... choose life, not death! But no one is wise enough or good enough to take it."[32]

---

[30] Grossman, 196.

[31] Glenn R. Schiraldi. *Post-Traumatic Stress Disorder Sourcebook*, (New York: McGraw Hill, 2009), xi.

[32] Charles L. Feinberg, "Jeremiah" in Isaiah, Jeremiah, Lamentations, Ezekiel, vol. 6 *The Expositors Bible Commentary*, ed. Frank E. Gaebelein (Grand Rapids: Zondervan, 2010), 259.

Man has the choice. Choose God and his omniscient ways or take the reins and take your chances. God presents us with an opportunity to let Him give us direction, as He sees ahead and knows what's coming. He will not force His way on us. It is our choice.

# Chapter 4

## Various Worldviews

Soldiers who lack a relationship with God do not possess needed insights into the reasoning behind the issues one can encounter in traumatic situations. Cultures in other lands will ask questions concerning the tragedy in their moralistic framework. When tragedies occur, perspective is important. Those of the Western mind might ask the God they suppose exists, "Why?" Others from the East will say it is a matter of karma, reflecting their Hindi or Buddhist worldview. As apologist Ravi Zacharias has noted, "The naturalist ought not to be raising the question as a moral problem, because in a naturalistic framework, morality is very subjective. So, in a real sense the only one who can justifiably raise the question is the one within the Judeo-Christian framework."[33] Trauma is compounded when a person's questions do not get answered when the Bible is taught and the Holy Spirit is not permitted to teach the unreceptive heart. The Bible answers questions to the satisfaction of the traumatized soldier. Surely a living human spirit energized by the presence of the

---

33  Zacharias. *Beyond Opinion: Living the Faith We Defend,* 180.

Holy Spirit shall make all the difference. As Solomon asks, "The spirit of a man shall sustain his infirmity, but a wounded spirit who can bear?" (Prov. 18:14). John declares, "And ye shall know the truth, and the truth shall make you free ... If the Son therefore shall make you free, ye shall be free indeed." (John 8:32, 36.) This concept, when the Holy Spirit applies the Word to the human soul, He will reduce the stress of trauma and begin the healing process. Those from other moralistic traditions are permitted to so frame the questions that their stresses can be answered away and nullified. Some that come from an eastern thought process, if they step out from under that umbrella of moral protection, could begin contending with those questions that the West struggles with now.

When stress is not relieved in a short amount of time, it can bring about mental, emotional, or physical trauma. The trauma then translates into various illnesses that require a doctor's care. Individuals have tried, but as Dr Schiraldi tells the reader, based on his psychology background admits, "As yet, no one treatment approach has been shown to be superior to any other for all people."[34] But he does not see things from God's perspective.

From the military standpoint using combat strategy, in war control is essential. When control is lost, the potential for trauma often ensues, fear engages, and ingrained training goes away. When control is lost, four general areas are affected: change in appetite, loss or even increase in sex drive, aggression, and isolation. Sometimes this is called fight or flight.

---

34  Schiraldi, xiii.

## The Return Home

When American World War II soldiers returned from combat "they returned as a unit together with the same guys they had spent the whole war with, on board a ship, spending weeks joking, laughing, gambling, and telling tall tales as they cooled down and depressurized in what psychologists would call a very supportive group-therapy environment on the long voyage home."[35] This gave a little time to adjust to home, family, and the slower pace of the noncombat environment. Today's soldier is not so treated but is home from the war in a matter of hours, flying first class on a luxury liner with little opportunity to recover from the incredible pressures and stressors of months at war. Coming back from Iraq, me and the unit all simply wanted to get caught up on sleep. Soldiers are rushed to train, rushed to war, and rushed home. No meaningful noncombat interaction. No blowing off steam. No self-examination of moral failures. No transition. Result: problems at home.

Deployment for a front-line soldier consists of long hours in austere conditions. For those that are in close combat, there is the moment-by-moment stress, not knowing where or when the next attack might come. One moment is quiet, and the next could find one in a firefight. Author Allen Clark states, "In thinking about the enemy movement the previous evening, a ground attack was imminent."[36] This continuously heightened state of alert brought on by the involuntary, continuous use of the adrenal glands that produce the adrenaline

---
35  Ibid., 286.
36  Allen Clark, *Wounded Soldier, Healing Warrior* (St Paul, MN; Zenith Press, 2007), 10.

needed for that heightened state of alert results in hypervigilance. Psychologist Glen Schiraldi further explains:

> Hypervigilance might be demonstrated as feeling vulnerable … unable to feel calm in safe places, feeling of repetition, anticipating disaster, such as needing to sit in the corner of a room with one's back to the wall while looking for exits … [r]apid scanning, looking over one's shoulder, keeping a weapon, being overprotective or over controlling. Exaggerated startle response means you are easily frightened."[37]

When the soldier leaves the war zone, the brain's function of supplying adrenaline for the body and mind's need can remain in a heightened alert condition. Schiraldi says, "PTSD is considered an anxiety disorder … anxiety is essentially worrisome thoughts plus excessive emotional and physical arousal."[38] When normal conditions of non-war scenarios occur, normal reactions are replaced by overreactions, which will take a toll on the soldier if the brain's condition is not adjusted. Other symptoms include physical fatigue and: "tension, fatigue, trembling, tingling, nausea, digestive tract problems, hyperventilation, pounding heart, suffocating feeling, panic attacks."[39]

The contemporary battle zone has intensified, and PTSD symptoms have increased due to extreme devastation brought on by the modern weapons of

---
37  Schiraldi, 9.
38  Ibid., 13.
39  Ibid., 14.

war. Modern warfare features weapons that add to the carnage.

> As history unfolded, science developed, and technology increased, the names of the war-induced afflictions and our strategies for responding to them, like war itself, became increasingly less humanistic, and more clinical and technical. What was once thought of as Godlike Wrath a soul piercing wound evolved through the millennia, finally becoming the PTSD we use today. And it is still changing.[40]

Medical Advancements

Surviving a physical injury means more PTSD (soulish injury). We now have advanced technology on the battlefield in both the weaponry that maim and kill, and life-saving techniques performed by medics within seconds of injury, in the emergency room, and in rehabilitation. Dean tells the reader, "Medicine was still an inexact science during the Civil War era, and the great advances in sanitation, germ theory, medical education and medical training, as well as the emergence of the hospital as the modern technological palace of healing, were in the future."[41] These life-saving techniques used at what is known as "the golden hour" allow soldiers to survive injuries that used to kill them. Whereas, now there are "advancements in medical technology and equipment that came out of the wars in Iraq and Afghanistan: Tourniquets [*were*]

---

40 Edward Tick, *Warrior's Return* (Boulder, Co: Sounds True, 2014), 143–144.
41 Dean, 51.

... used since the Civil War ... constricting the flow of traumatic bleeding [*resulting in loss of limbs*]. [*And*] ... nearly fifty percent of combat death since World War II can be attributed to blood loss."[42] Today, advancements include the golden hour blood containers kept safely at the thirty-four to forty-three degrees Fahrenheit range needed for a transfusion. Now, with an increase in survival rates comes the issue of helping the mind cope with the trauma it has experienced. For example, a soldier may have seen the body of a fellow soldier blown up while they escaped death because of quick use of medical aid. Besides this, the individual may be part of the clean-up team, bagging the pieces that remain of their buddy.

Medical procedures on the battlefield at the point of contact have resulted in saved lives. Wounds once considered lethal are now often handled routinely on the spot. Soldiers who had once been casualties of war are now rescued from death through immediate medical treatment, rehabilitated, and able to resume life; albeit, with a missing limb or some other injury, or even prosthetics. The services wish to keep as many war vets available to stay in the fight, "Six percent of service members wounded in Iraq experienced amputations. Advancements in prosthetics include the developments of robotic prosthetics and vacuum-assisted suction sockets for hip disarticulation."[43] Some soldiers even return to the war zone. "More than 250 service

---

42  Andrea Signor, "Advancements in Medical Technology," www.taskandpurpose.com Oct. 2014.
43  Andrea Signor. "Advancements in Medical Technology."

members with amputation returned to active duty and more than fifty deployed again."[44]

Injuries that once killed are now the reason survivors have to cope with a wounded spirit that need treatment. The recent signature wound of the modern wars has been traumatic brain injury or TBI. "In 2012, … hyperbaric oxygen therapy … exposes patients to pure oxygen, increasing the amount of oxygen red blood cells and body tissue absorbed, which, in theory, can change the way the body heals."[45] Medical treatments have included medications for the emotional issues that soldiers have encountered. However, with the use of anything, there can come abuses. Some years back, an opioid epidemic had been declared. Millions of civilians and military personnel are overprescribed medications for almost any reason. This abuse of opioids has brought the Department of Defense to reconsider the services rendered by their military doctors. Recently, an opioid workshop, opened to the public, at a military installation took place with the spokesman for integrative Pain Management spoke. He spoke to the three of us who were in attendance from that community. In attempting to help the military communities recognize the problem of overprescribing of medications, suicides, and other problems throughout the military, the lack of attention and participation is an indicator of the lack of concern for those problems was brought to the forefront.

Military members have answered the call to engage the enemy in conflicts around the world, but they have

---

44   Ibid.
45   Ibid.

returned forever changed by the stressors they have faced. These soldiers are encouraged to get assistance to adjust with the help of family members, behavioral professionals, and even clergy. A quality support system is essential. Unfortunately, in the American culture Christian spirituality has been neglected.

## How to conduct a war, in the field and in the soul

Another aspect of the increase in PTSD is the way modern wars are conducted. Between the World Wars, the new and expanding practice of night warfare brought forth the necessity of a military regulation governing it. In CMH Pub 104–3 Night Combat, the directives were written on how to conduct night operations and in what circumstances such actions would be permissible. The manual instructs, "During two world wars, night and other periods of low visibility, such as fog, snowstorm or rainstorm gradually came to be considered the ideal time for action."[46] With that, the war changed in its technologies. Daylight fighting was all the soldier knew for many thousands of years. During the daylight or full moons, soldiers would fight. The night was for sleeping and the opportunity to rest themselves on a more regular schedule and eat a decent meal. Soldiers would discuss the day's events and be able to debrief one another without even explaining what they were experiencing. Each soldier shared with other soldiers what they were thinking, and each knew they were not alone in their experiences.

---

46   US War Department, Night Combat. Replaces DA Pamphlet 2–236, June 1953.

According to written accounts, the chaplain would help the American Civil War soldier with his spiritual issues. Soldiers that had an acumen toward the spiritual were able to get instruction from the clergy who themselves put on the uniform. Chaplains helped soldiers through difficult times and were often leaders of their hometown units. Historian and author Charles Pitts describes it this way, "When the call to arms rang through the South, the pastors were among the first and most enthusiastic to respond ... into the ranks stepped the 'men of the cloth.'"[47] Chaplains would also be available to conduct services for the soldiers, giving the frontline fighter a needed spiritual perspective of the events that the soldiers were experiencing around them. Chaplains, in order to help the then called Soldier's Heart, PTSD-afflicted soldier, must themselves believe in the spiritual efficacy of the Bible. "The word 'trauma' is from the Greek word which means 'a wounding.'"[48] So trauma (PTSD) is a wound, only invisible.

What has happened in post-World War II America brought about a new philosophy within the culture that a new view on PTSD therapies is currently developing. The scenarios and mind-set have changed. Since the introduction into the American culture of rock music and others with the Eastern mysticism religions via the Beatles, introducing "Maharishi Mahesh Yogi and practiced his Transcendental Meditation (TM) style of Yoga. When it was brought to the West, Maharishi called it the 'Spiritual Regeneration Movement' ...

---

47 Charles F. Pitts. *Chaplains in Gray* (Nashville: Broadman Press, 1957), 26.
48 Chris Adsit, *The Combat Trauma Healing Manual* (Newport News, VA: Military Ministry Press, 2007), 23.

after the influence of Eastern mysticism over the past forty years, nearly everyone wants to be 'spiritual', but not religious."[49] Mansfield observed, "Suddenly, America seems to be wrestling with the role religion has to play in her military culture ... America is a nation religiously in tension with itself ... institutions of American government are required under force of recent Supreme Court decisions to lean religiously neutral if not secular."[50] For an example, says Gould:

> The Army has taken a step toward officially acknowledging humanism among other faiths and beliefs systems, ending years of resistance to the idea, advocates say. The faith code for humanism—a secular philosophy that emphasizes humanity and not divinity—was official approved by the service alongside Muslim, Hindu, Wiccan, Jewish, Buddhist and various Christian denominations.[51]

In deciding to keep faith with religious freedom, those who are in the position to make decisions have relabeled service members choosing the "no preference" category (in which there are 276, 000 or one in four servicemembers, while another 13,000 are atheist or agnostic) can now be labeled "humanist."[52]

---

49  Dave Hunt, *Yoga and the Body of Christ* (Bend, OR; Harvest House, 2006), 55, Kindle.
50  Stephen Mansfield, *The Faith of the American Soldier* (New York: Penguin, 2005), 11.
51  Joe Gould, Army Recognizes 'Humanism' as a Religious Preference, Army Times, May 5, 2014, 18.
52  New York Times. 1972. "U.S. Court Rejects Mandatory Chapel at Service Schools." Accessed August 13, 2018. http://www.nytimes.com.

This process toward official recognition of humanism is the final official declaring of where the United States is in mind if not in action. Tolerance leans toward the approval of humanism at the expense of Christianity. Tolerance moves us toward the lowest common denominator and away from Christ and the gospel. We see this in action in the military service academies where the officers train, no longer require chapel. Stahl comments, "The United States Court of Appeals for the District of Columbia ruled today, 2–1, that compulsory chapel attendance at the United States military academies was an unconstitutional violation of the First Amendment's guarantee of freedom of religion."[53] When services members look to their leadership in combat to have a faith perspective on war and its challenges, the academies remove the religious option and by insinuation tell those who serve it is not important. Further moving them toward the option of being spiritual without being religious. This decision leaves our military spiritually defenseless in war and in life.

---

[53]

# CHAPTER 5

## The Importance of the Mind

It is imperative to understand the current beliefs that affect how health professionals are pursuing channels of relief for those who are plagued by PTSD. "Within American society, PTSD has proven to have devastating effects. According to Sidran Institute the economic burden of PTSD is large."[54] Accumulated statistics from an online provider who has compiled information stating, "the annual cost to society of anxiety disorders is estimated to be significantly over $42.3 billion, often due to misdiagnosis and under treatment."[55] According to Sidran, the comorbidity that plague those with PTSD and the repeated use of services drive up costs. Repeated visits for anxiety disorder treatment reflects the largest component. Success rates have been researched, and no definitive results can be located. What has been stated above is a good indicator of the ongoing targeting of the temporary relief of symptoms rather than a solution to the problem.

---

54 AAACEUs Introduction PTSD Statistics According to Sidran. Accessed 12 May 2020.
55 Ibid.

## Leaving Christianity Behind

A gradual shift in the religious perspectives in American culture and how they affect the philosophy of those in the various arenas of health care are a telling sign of what is being emphasized for a PTSD cure. In pursuing the examination of the drift away from biblical Christianity toward the main centers of supposed relief, psychology and pharmaceuticals, will be examined in their various facets. Psychology, by strict definition, would be a study of the soul. Many, from literature to mesmerism to the established sciences, dismiss Christianity and its popular theology and found ways to rework the doctrine of God in other ways of understanding mankind. The fields mentioned have stepped in and have been accepted by society as plausible avenues of study that include neurology and even theology. Societies have deferred to the increasingly secular science to redefine the areas belonging to mental health. "Through the years prior to the twentieth century the word psychology, as mentioned, had to do with the study of the soul, primarily from the theological perspective. The conflicting ideas about the nature of the will, inner motivations, passions, and reasons were argued from various biblical perspectives."[56] As theological studies about man increased, the study of the soul took on greater significance and took on greater importance than the study of God. Friedrich Schleiermacher, a German theologian and an advocate of the increasingly influential higher criticism that questions the veracity

---

56 Martin and Deidre Bobgan, *Against Biblical Counseling for the Bible* (Santa Barbara: EastGate Pub, 1994), 35.

of the Bible, began including self-consciousness into his theology. With this understanding, the subjective experience took a more significant role in his teaching. Later, mental philosophy and natural theology joined forces. Natural science and philosophy that keyed on man's mental ability began influencing theology to bring it to a place where it was ready to merge into psychology as it is known today.

The medical community has researched these areas of PTSD and has developed some new approaches that appear to be helping many, at least in the short-term. According to Julie Revelant in EverydayHealth.com, some therapies are finding favorable results:

> In 2013, briefly after joining the National Guard, Anderson was medically discharged as a result of his PTSD diagnosis. Although he had tried other types of treatments, he learned about accelerated resolution therapy (ART), and after just one session, his intrusive memories disappeared. "ART for me has been like brain fitness on steroids," he says.
>
> According to a March 2017 study in the journal *Current Psychiatry Reports,* although early research suggests ART may be an effective therapy for PTSD, there has been only one randomized controlled trial to date, so more research is needed.[57]

---

57  Julie Revelant, "How Trauma in the Military can Lead to PTSD and how to Find Relief for You and Your Loved Ones" www.EverydayHealth.com, 20 April, 2018.

Reconsolidation Treatment of Memories (RMT) research is claiming a ninety percent success rate for those who stick with their program. It consists of:

3 to 4, ninety-minute therapy sessions.

Sessions are clinician-led during which the client sits in a comfortable chair and visualizes pictures on an imagined movie screen in a way that separates the traumatic memories from the traumatic feelings.

The sessions require no homework or practice outside the therapy sessions.

Clients remain completely relaxed and comfortable while they construct the images on the imagined movie screen during the treatments.

The treatments completely eliminate traumatic nightmares, flashback and directly related emotional problems for over 90% of clients.

After RTM therapy, people can remember past traumatic events with no traumatic feelings.[58]

> The goals include: Alleviate flashbacks and nightmares. Eliminate re-living stressful events, including negative physical reactions like sweating, muscular tensions and heart pounding. Improved sleep, concentration, emotional control. Reduced hyper-vigilance.
>
> Increased freedom in thought and action.[59]

The program is not explained in specifics, but rather gives overview and results. These are just a couple of

---
58   www.rtmtrainingcenter.com, 2020.
59   Ibid.

the programs available for those who are diagnosed as victims of PTSD.

Further studies done by National Institutes of Health, National Library of Medicine, and the National Center for Biotechnology Information show the most highly recommended therapies for PTSD: Prolonged Exposure (PE) therapy, Cognitive Processing Therapy (CPT), and Cognitive Behavior Therapy (CBT). PE attempts to remove the fear factor from the traumatic event. Facing fears by simply removing bad information will not do. It must be replaced with new information that best fits the truth of the traumatic event. These exercises are accompanied with breathing exercise that helps the thinking process. Living and thoughts (in vivo and imaginal) encounters are faced and processing trauma is taught. CPT is used when a traumatized person attempts to answer the reasons for an event. Often, they will blame themselves for why the event happened. CPT attempts to shift personal beliefs to answer the traumatic event. CBT is applied when a traumatic event is thought out in a different way, bringing about a differing result that lessens the guilt factor for the victim. Many times, this is achieved by writing out a new narrative. These three areas of therapy are highly recommended in the psychology community. "The aggregate proportion of dropout across all active treatments was 18.28%."[60] The Men's Legal Center located near the San Diego Naval Station at Coronado and near Marine Corps Camp Pendleton reports on their website, "According to the latest numbers released by the Pentagon, 21,290 of the 689,060 active married

---

60  www.ncbi.nim.mih.gov/pmc.

military personnel divorced during the last fiscal year. That's a divorce rate of between 3 and 3.1 percent. Hidden in those numbers is the revelation that female troops are divorcing at a higher rate than their male counterparts. For example, the divorce rate among women in the US Army is 275 percent higher than men."[61]

It is estimated that fifty percent of marriages of military members with PTSD end in divorce. Separations stem from domestic violence, substance abuse associated with attempts at PTSD relief, and suicides and attempted suicides. One important element to the relief of stress on the family's part is to realize that the military member's stress and possible PTSD is not the family members' fault. The civilian spouse need not take the blame for it. Also, they can find ways through chaplains or medical practitioners and other counselors to understand how stress brought on by the military member can be addressed and how they can have a part in relieving the trauma symptoms.

The workplace can be challenging for those with PTSD. Employers who hire someone with PTSD must be aware of the possibility of job disruption if the work environment involves noise, sudden movements, or things that could startle the average worker. Sudden and startling events could bring about flashbacks, panic attacks, or worse from one whose background includes such perceived life-threatening events. "Managers and co-workers can support employees with PTSD

---

61  "What's the Divorce Rate Among Military Personnel?" Men's Legal Center, accessed 12 May, 2020, www.menslegal.com.

by demonstrating patience and understanding. The resulting negative behaviors and impaired performance at work are not entirely in the person's control."[62]

The above therapies deriving from the medical and psychological communities are helpful to some extent for some, while others find little or no relief. Since the goal of this book is not to resolve problems temporarily but eternally through faith in the Lord Jesus Christ, the ultimate source from all trauma is through faith in the Christian Savior, Jesus. He alone can solve all problems in this life on a moment-by-moment and day-by-day basis and then finally solve all problems for eternity in heaven where God will provide a glorified mind and body for every Christian, thus removing all weaknesses and human frailties.

Our goal should be to increase in the knowledge of God concerning PTSD and to share the findings with those struggling with PTSD, thus bettering ministry opportunities among those who need assistance, along with assisting medical and mental health professionals, who show concern and understand the truth of God's Word, to see the possible dangers of some practices used within their profession. Implementing sound Bible teaching will help the soldier and family member(s), and health professionals, to find personal spiritual growth through Bible study, Bible meditation, and prayer with emphasis upon a solid biblical presentation of the gospel.

The military has been seeking answers to the issues of PTSD, and the spiritual aspects has been researched by many chaplains. In researching this problem, finding

---

62  A Primer for Employers, www.workplacementalhealth.org.

biblical answers, and sharing them with the PTSD diagnosed soldier, efforts are being made to increase the effectiveness of treatments. It has not yet become clear if what the chaplains have attempted has worked as well as they wished.

Being aware of the issues that the nation's healers are working to overcome causes me to double my efforts in learning how to solve the real problem of the spirit. As learning increases about the true issues of the traumatized soul and spirit, this information needs to be shared with those who are in need of learning and putting it to use. The fear and anxiety and other issues that are plaguing warriors are proving to be only temporarily solved by psychology and by drugs.

The benefit of concurrent drug use with the proposed Bible study would be in temporary doses in order to stabilize the patient so that there is an opportunity to explain the gospel and the power of God. It might also show the uselessness of long-term drug use. In personal and professional training aspects, many secular counselors may not recognize the effectiveness of the Bible, but as many wounded spirits come under God's healing hand, it will become evident the soldiers' emotional healing has happened. The true answers that came from the Word of God will be obvious, and God will be glorified. These three goals, once applied, should be shared with other ministers who will stand by the Bible to help soldiers solve their problems.

Study of God's Word through this book will encourage those without Jesus Christ to repent of sin and confess Christ as Savior and then gain spiritual fitness through Bible memory and Bible meditation of key Scriptures that refer to the need for Bible meditation in making the difference in the recovery of the heart (the meditator). These will help calm and clear thinking of the mind, the will, and the emotions (the soul). Psalm 1:2 and Joshua 1:8 begin the references, along with the verses in Psalm 119, especially verses 11, 15, 23, 34, 48, 78, 97, 99, and 148. They speak of the importance of day and night meditation on the Bible so that the person will think right, make good choices, do right, and have successful results. God's Word promises it. A veteran was helped, who had a testimony that by playing the Word of God during the night *while sleeping* helped him after suffering with nightmares and otherwise experiencing very restless nights. He testified to receiving complete relief from his reoccurring night haunts. He now sleeps all night and wakes feeling refreshed. The body may sleep, but the mind and the soul are always awake.

**Setting Goals for Yourself**

The most important concept to grasp includes the PTSD victims' need for salvation in Jesus Christ and, through salvation in Christ, find spiritual relief from their wounded spirit, as the Spirit is then able to minister to bring comfort as they discover the "peace that passeth all understanding" (Phil 4:7a). Choosing to trust Christ is the starting point to any discipleship program, which will also include other aspects of how a better understanding of the Christian life and God's involvement in it can bring relief from the trauma soldiers have experienced in war. To assist those in reaching their goal, that of spiritual healing of trauma is, First, through the use of key Scripture passages that by reading and meditating allow God to speak to the individual about their particular needs. Then the person can choose to do whatever guidance might be given by the verse being meditated upon as part of his/her healing. Second, an effective program will encourage spiritual fitness through Bible memory that stems from Bible study and prayer. Meditation is most effective done individually with a paper and pen ready to write down what God reveals to you. The Third goal could be to prepare better those who are dealing with stress to know and utilize the attributes of the all-present and all-powerful God. Fourth, a good goal is that through Bible knowledge, the soldier can share his faith, knowing how to lead another to the Christ for salvation with others so that the one who shares can strengthen his/her own faith at the same time. By enhancing others' spiritual growth, I personally may be more effective in this ministry in reaching out to not only the military communities, but it may extend beyond to other soldiers, dependents, and veterans in other locations to help them biblically overcome PTSD.

The most important thing to remember is that when the PTSD sufferer becomes born again the Holy Spirit will be inside that individual to minister the Word of God as it is applied to the spiritual wound. The invisible wound, this wounded spirit, can only be healed from within. Paul expressed the internal workings of God in Philippians when he wrote: "My God shall supply all your need according to his riches in glory by Christ Jesus" (Phil. 4:19). In 1 Peter 5:10, Peter expounds: "But the God of all grace, who hath called us unto his eternal glory by Christ Jesus, after that ye suffered a while, make you perfect, stablish, strengthen, settle you." I am available through information in the back of this book to conduct biblical/pastoral counseling with the soldiers and/or family members in any area they may have questions. This book is intended to assist in the recovery from PTSD—or help soldiers avoid PTSD through studies in pertinent Scripture passages that have to do with the issues traumatized soldiers often face. By meditation upon these Scriptures and obedience to them, the soldier's spirit will, by the indwelling Holy Spirit, receive needed instruction for the soul, allowing God to work.

I will later speak on the different issues that soldiers face and how God can make a difference in their lives. It is important to understand the power of the Scriptures that God speaks through and recognize the love that He has for mankind despite the pain that one has been experienced. He has a plan for every one of His children that will not fail. As the PTSD sufferer begins understanding where God is in his suffering, he will realize that God is not the inflictor, but rather the healer through Christ. An ongoing reliance on God and the Bible will bring a coping relief when those stressful moments occur. PTSD will not see full resolution in this life, for it will be a constant battle that can be won each hour through God's Word being continually applied to the wound. God will provide help to the sufferer through the Scriptures and the ministry of the

Holy Spirit without the side effects or addictive nature that accompany drugs. This fact is the beginning of the removal of the power of PTSD. Some topics will be covered, such as anxiety, fear of the future, and even fear of death, and forgiveness of all guilt and sin (even those sins that one might not be aware of), and how one finds peace. These issues and others are answered in the person of the Lord Jesus Christ through this book. Because fear is a major issue to those with PTSD, a helpful verse is "Fear thou not; I am with thee: be not dismayed; for I am thy God: I will strengthen thee; yea, I will help thee; yea, I will uphold thee with the right hand of my righteousness" (Isa. 41:10).

Who is God? What's he like? These are important questions to ask because your answer will determine to what extent you will trust Him. The greater the trust, the more the PTSD sufferer can be aware of what God can offer in resolving trauma. If there is a greater trust in medications than of God, that is where you will go to find relief. After, you, the soldier, gain the awareness of what God can do for you, the lessons He has for you will begin. Using the Word, God gives ways to solve and avoid further episodes of PTSD.

In clarification, patients refraining from pharmaceutical drugs, thinking they will be helpful in relieving emotional issues, such as anxiety, depression, and so forth, find drug's usefulness is only temporary. I refer only to those drugs that alter emotional states. Some drugs assist the body to maintain normal functions but are not being produced by the body, such as insulin. Drugs taken for emotional purposes are to be avoided. I *do not* recommend to anyone who is currently on any medications through a physician's prescription that they remove themselves from such medications without the assistance of that physician. Along with gaining an assessment of your spiritual condition, it would be wise to get a thorough physical exam to determine if there are any areas in which a physician's help might be gained.

## Conclusion

This book is intended to assist you, be you military or civilian who are struggling with PTSD, by guiding you to allow God to assist with solving the challenges you face. This book is designed to expose historical information of PTSD's origins and draw biblical findings of how these issues came about, as well as what has been done to try to relieve them. It will also show various methods, which have worked or failed to work and what is the best way forward when it comes to God applying his healing touch. I show from the Bible what most effectively ministers to those who have experienced the emotional traumas that are primarily due to war. In understanding the biblical way to treat PTSD, it will be crucial to realize that the alternative methods used by modern psychology and by social services may provide temporary relief from symptoms but will not confront root problems and may bring about more significant issues in the future. It is best to refrain from psychology. It is also important to comprehend that to work in cooperation with the mental health or medical personnel can only be done to the extent that the attending physician agrees that the Bible has answers where the doctor's wisdom leaves off. The sad truth is that the biblical approach and the modern professional behavioral health and medical approach have often been opposed to one another. The Bible should be adhered to where they differ. Working independently, one-on-one with individuals or with small groups of PTSD sufferers will probably be most effective.

# Chapter 6

## Various Aspects of Remedies for PTSD

In developing a Bible-based plan of treatment, I intend to undergird this book with the King James Version of the Bible and various commentaries. I believe that improvements can be made in therapy by implementing biblical teaching in lieu of some of the current psychological and medicinal answers suggested by the psychological and medical communities. I will explore and expose in this section the various ways in which society has come about to offer new and different ways to provide therapies. God's Word has always been the spiritual remedy, and while many others in the medical arena have helped to a degree in the physical area, in the spiritual, they have attempted to intrude with their own views. The spiritual is God's area, and unfortunately many have fallen into the trap of confusing the medicinal or mental health for the spiritual. As you will see, there have been a strange mixture of mental–spiritual, and even social attempts at healing our ills.

Many therapies have been implemented and do appear to bring some measure of relief to those who partake of them. Improvement in the spiritual arena, however, comes not only in this life but in that which is to come. A temporary solution in this life can be obtained at times by certain therapies; however, some therapies, as will be discussed below, will end in eternal death because the treatment fails to include salvation in Jesus Christ, which the Bible teaches is the only way to heaven. Trained psychologist and now a biblical counselor Martin Bobgan warns, "With the rising interest in studying the mind and soul, there was a gradual shift from learning about creation (including mankind) through knowing the Creator to studying creation by other means."[63]

## New Age and Eastern Practices and various ways of leaving the Truth: A Brief History

Hypnotism has become part of the pre-psychology mind-set since the early1900's. Bobgan instructs in the hypnotic origins saying, "Hypnosis has been used as a method of mental, emotional, behavioral, and physical healing for hundreds and even thousands of years. Witchdoctors, Sufi practitioners, shamans, Hindus, Buddhists, and yogis have practiced hypnosis, and now medical doctors, dentists, psychotherapists, and others have joined them."[64] Mesmerism of the 1700s was first called animal magnetism by Anton Mesmer in 1779. It became labeled as mesmerism by Scottish physician James Braid in the 1840s, later hypnosis, and later yet under modifications, psychotherapy. The removal of magnets were part and parcel of the technique as a

---

63 Bobgan, *Against Biblical Counseling for the Bible*, 35–36.
64 Martin Bobgan, *Hypnosis: Medical, Scientific or Occultic* (Santa Barbara: EastGate Publishing, 2001), 5.

person would have magnets passed over them as they sat in a tub, according to Jan Ehrenwald,65 Mesmer believed an ethereal fluid was responsible for the linking of animate and inanimate objects, which connected to stars that operated through Mesmer. His hypothesis was linked to astrology and magic, according to Ehrenwald.

Sigmund Freud borrowed from these ideas and gets much of the credit for the psychology of today, but Freud borrowed from those, such as Jonathan Edwards. Edwards preached the nearness of God and the infused life; that comfort and joy would be available to all through God. Freud redefined Edwards's God, explains Fuller, saying, "This notion was open to appealing interpretation."[66] A new American spirituality emerged through the literature by Coleridge, Emerson, and James; some proclaimed them as the beginnings of the modern beliefs of Jehovah's Witnesses, Mormons, and Christian Scientists. For many, the new spirituality also came with an increase in the standard of living and a feeling of superiority. Fuller records, "For Emerson, religion has its foundation in the act of becoming inwardly receptive to the Over-Soul. The self—like the Hindu Atman—was a succession of layers or sheaths. Only by peeling away the outer sheaths can one hope to become a 'vehicle of the divine principle that lurks within.'"[67] Fuller goes further, using Ahlstrom's account stating that religion of harmony comes from economic and physical health and adds to harmony with the

---

65 Jan Ehrenwald, ed. *The History of Psychotherapy.* (Northvale, NJ: Jason Aronson, Inc., 1991), 221.
66 Robert C. Fuller. *Americans and the Unconscious* (New York: Oxford, 1986), 14.
67 Fuller, 15.

cosmos. Fuller claims, "The deity—here conceived as an indwelling cosmic force—is approached not via petitionary prayer or acts of worship, but through a series of inner adjustments."[68] A further philosophy is that divinity is flowing through every physical object; man is a part of God, and God is a part of man. This sort of influence into new ways of thinking along religious lines coupled with greater invention assisted man's thinking toward a prideful outlook, along with a new feeling of freedom from God later coined the "gilded age." Fuller adds, "This also seems true for many intellectuals in the 1880s and 1890s."[69]

Concerning the material culture, Kordas states, "The Gilded Age is often remembered as an age of material excess. Not only did the sheer numbers of everyday goods exceed those produced in earlier periods, so too did the complexity, specialization, and elaboration of common goods."[70] The Gilded Age brought convenience, luxury, and a displaced view on religion that would prove to bring increasing self-reliance, leaving faith in God behind. Along with a material increase in America came an increase in immigration from Europe and China. The philosophies of Darwinism were aided by Herbert Spencer who coined the phrase "survival of the fittest." Carl Sandburg wrote about "the city he loves is stormy, husky, brawling."[71] The word *husky* was used to describe attitudes that were big, tough, and strong, and *brawling* referred to the violence exhibited

---

68 Ibid., 18.
69 Ibid., 19.
70 Rodney P. Carlisle Gen Ed. *Handbook to Look in America: The Gilded Age* (New York: Infobase Pub, 2009), 37.
71 Carlisle, 55.

in society on an increasing scale. This attitude gave a push toward reliance on the sciences as they expanded in the inventions of the day. Darwinian evolution, having been on the scene for a couple of decades, became increasingly popular, and the belief that man was getting better and smarter increased in medicines, communications, transportation, and women's rights, among others.

The Irish Catholics, who had come to settle in America, began influencing American thinking and added to the social gospel that was gaining credence. Jewish migration was also an element, along with the ethical cultural movement (ECM), begun by a German Rabbi, Felix Adler. Bill Kte'pi explains, "All religions included ethical truths, ECM said, and following ethical principles was the path to wisdom and enlightenment. ECM makes no appeals at all to supernatural authority."[72] This society was the beginning of other ethical communities, such as the National Association for the Advancement of Colored People (NAACP) and other groups, such as Jehovah's Witnesses, Christian Science, and the Church of Jesus Christ of Latter-Day Saints (Mormons). Along came the belief that God no longer existed in the same way as the old Protestant view. Christian styles of religion were pushed to the side. Philosophers, such as William Graham Sumner among others, influenced education. With the increase in secularism came increasing problems. Carlisle adds, "Part of the task which devolves on those who are subject to the duty is to define the problem. They are told only that something is the matter: that it behooves them to

---

72   Ibid., 108.

find out what it is, and how to correct it, and then to work out the cure."[73] With each philosophy comes a different view of various answers to life's problems. As mentioned, many cults arose; these along with liberal churches increasingly questioned the Bible, bringing in a social gospel. A new way arose to solve problems of the mind. Enter Sigmund Freud. Opinions on Freud vary, with such statements as:

> Sigmund Freud was a genius, Sigmund Freud was a fraud. Sigmund Freud was a man of letters, or perhaps a philosopher, or a cryptic-biologist. Sigmund Freud discovered psychoanalysis by delving deep into his own dreams and penetrating the mysteries of his patients. Sigmund Freud stole most of his good ideas from others and invented the rest out of his own odd imagination. Freud was the maker of a new science of the mind that dominated the west for much of the twentieth century. Freud was an unscientific conjurer who created a mass delusion.[74]

Others, such as Hunt, declare, "Freud has been exposed as a fraud. His work was not scientific. Some of the case studies he offered to support his theories are disguised autobiographical sketches. His 'discoveries' reflect his own perverted sexual obsessions."[75] Freud's predecessors include Henry Ward Beecher and

---

73 Fuller, 56.
74 George Makari, *Revolution in Mind* (New York: Harper Collins, 2008), 3.
75 Dave Hunt, *Occult Invasion* (Eugene, OR: Harvest House, 1998), 447–448.

Horace Bushnell. While they were writing, others "were busily investigating these uncharted mental territories. Nature—or, more precisely, psychological nature—was thought to contain the mechanism for the harmonization of the individual selves with the World Spirit."[76] This thinking included new thought, theosophy, and spiritualism.

As mentioned earlier, Anton Mesmer postulated a view that an invisible fluid was present throughout the universe that he termed animal magnetism. Other theories inspired his students to expand his thought to cause some students to follow Mesmer's techniques, where some would fall into a sleeplike state. Fuller says, "They had, so to speak, become 'mesmerized.'"[77] Phineas Quimby was a successful mesmerist in the early 1800s. His practices in animal magnetism were showing astonishing results. Quimby became prolific in healings through the mesmerism practice when his practices were less expensive, resulting in the same healing effect. Quimby, however, had gone in a different direction, theorizing that the individual mind played a far greater role than many before had hypothesized.

Fuller asserts, "Quimby moved mesmerism one step closer to modern psychology by specifically identifying ideas—not magnetic fluids—as the root cause of both physical and emotional disorders. In Quimby's words, "all sickness is in the mind or belief … to cure the disease is to correct the error, destroy the cause, and the effect will cease.'"[78] Quimby would become a bridge from

---
76  Fuller, 26.
77  Ibid., 31.
78  Ibid., 47.

religion to the irreligious psychology sciences. Fuller observes, "Quimby also psychologized the Protestant ethic. His philosophy of mind-cure continued to affirm the intimate connection between religious conviction and material prosperity but shifted inward the realm in which one is to be held accountable. The mind-cure approach to religious and material well-being supported the democratic vision according to everyone exercising dominion over his or her own psychological realm."[79] This philosophy of mental and physical health, combined with the materialism of the upcoming gilded age, fit together nicely, but it was not biblical.

Quimby's ideas soon spread throughout New England and became the precursor to today's psychology. Fuller ends with this observation, "For some Quimby's science of mind cure proved that physical universe contains a mystical dimension. For others, it bespoke self-help techniques for better adjusting oneself to the demands of everyday living. For still others, it promised a kind of high-powered telepathy by which to employ magical forces. But for all, mesmerist psychology had come to imply that the key to personal well-being lies within oneself."[80] The self-help philosophy is what appears to be the driving force behind modern psychology's attempt to help our troops suffering from PTSD today.

Freud brought a devious twist to his humanism, as Bobgan notes, "A number of explanations of how and why Freud came up with such unusual theories as those of infantile sexuality and the Oedipus complex have

---
79  Fuller, 48–49.
80  Ibid., 49.

been suggested. Many believe them to be the result of Freud's own distorted childhood and his own mental-emotional disturbances."[81] To some, he was a savior for mental health philosophy, to others an inventor of fairy tales, desperately searching for a replacement for the confining views of Scripture. Though others could have been given credit for the things that Freud developed, the time seemed to be ripe for new and different philosophies that better related to the changing times that were affecting morals and religious views in Europe.

The turn of the century became a time when many questioned Church fathers and their beliefs. The abandonment of some crucial areas of faith brought about an opening to what would become psychology. Makari agrees saying, "Religious beliefs regarding inner life would prove durable and influential, but during the second half of the nineteenth century such notions began to lose some credence, and in that ceded ground a science of mental life took root."[82] Gaining an understanding of what happened in the age of Freud and others helps in the understanding of today's psychology surge. The French Catholic church did not have the answers to what was taking place in their country, and when new technologies emerged, along with a lost war and revised economic thought, came a desire to look into a new way of thinking about humanity. Those looking for relief would go to some supposed healing away from God toward science, and others tended toward materialism and hedonism. In

---

81   Bobgan, *The End of Christian Psychology* (Santa Barbara: Eastgate Pub, 1997), 136–137.
82   Makari, 9.

attempting to replace pain with pleasure, many would seek out new and different forms of entertainment in escape from pain that also came meaninglessness in pleasure.

Psychiatrists prescribe pharmaceuticals in an attempt to provide an answer to physical pain and various mental trauma. Zacharias explains, there was an "inescapable existential reality: meaninglessness does not come from being weary of pain but from being weary of pleasure."[83] Then there are those who are attempting to combine science and pleasure through narcotics. The attempt in America to legalize marijuana, which is being successful to this point, is another attempt to avoid pain at all costs, especially when it can be legalized, seen as relief of a declared disability, and the government will pay for the prescription. A recent report from Scott Wilson states, "Plastic caps to hypodermic needles [*are*] tossed aside by scores of heroin addicts who dwell outside Twitter and Banana Republic and City Hall. The local government distributes them free to protect drug users from disease."[84]

---

83 Zacharias, *Beyond Opinion,* 206.
84 Scott Wilson, "San Francisco, rich and poor, turns to simple street solutions that underscore the city's complexities." *Washington Post* (September 3, 2018). http://www.washingtonpost.com/ (accessed September 4, 2018).

# CHAPTER 7

## Which brings us to today

Many in pharmaceuticals are promoting drug use without a concern for the drugs' uselessness. They try to help people obtain a feel-good attitude toward treatments. Peele advises: "The paradox of the American addiction treatment industry is the tremendous growth it maintains without demonstrating that it works."[85] Today, in America, with the emphasis on the betterment of man through human means, nearly all the soldiers, when returning from war, are processed through Behavior Health and can meet with a psychologist upon request. Often, when seen by a psychiatrist, patients are diagnosed with PTSD and prescribed medications, which often includes pain relief medication. With the increased medical attention has come an increase in those seeking prescription drugs to deal with their diagnosed PTSD. With the increase in prescriptions has come an increase in abuses. Abuses from addictions and supplemental income are shown based on congressional hearings testimony. Sisk

---

85  Stanton Peele, *Diseasing of America* (Lexington, MA: Lexington Books, 1989), 231.

observes, "The House Veterans Affairs Committee heard testimony Wednesday that was both encouraging and disturbing about PTSD programs and allegations that some vets are faking symptoms to get a disability check."[86] This faking often stems from the opportunity to see an added income for to the soldier through a disability rating.

Psychiatry/psychology and pharmaceuticals blend at this point to make a stronger and usually impenetrable link. The Diagnostic and Statistical Manual (DSM) from The American Psychological Association (APA) began recognizing PTSD in 1980. Once officially placed into the DSM as a disorder, the military saw a way to begin granting psychological services for that problem. Quickly the psychologists began developing their program for a "cure" that included psychiatrists, medication prescription capabilities, and medical doctors. There is a danger of overprescribed drugs that could bring on drug addiction and abuse. Psychologizing began, as Bobgan explains: "By psychologizing we mean teaching, trusting, and promoting unscientific and unproven psychological opinions in areas where the Bible has already spoken."[87] Since the time of psychologists, such as Freud, Jung, Adler, Maslow, Allport, Rogers, Glasser, Skinner, and others, the Bible has been downplayed and seen as archaic and out of date. Psychologist Thomas Szasz notes that, "The birth of psychiatry occurs when the study of the human soul is transferred from religion to

---

86    Richard Sisk, Some Vets with PTSD Are Scamming the VA: Testimony. Military.com, 8 Jun, 2017.

87    Martin and Deidre Bobgan, *PsychoHeresyPsychoHeresy* (Santa Barbara: EastGate Publishers, 2012), 8.

medicine, when the cure of soul becomes the treatment of mental diseases, and most importantly, when the repression of the heretic-madman ceases to be within the jurisdiction of the priest and becomes the province of the psychiatrist."[88]

When the church should have seen heresy coming and warned their people of the dangers, psychology entered into society and invaded the church. When pastors should have guided their people into how the Bible can answer their questions and solve their problems, ministers began to refer members to those in the psychology field of mental health. The Bible warns not to rely on those who are presenting a new philosophy when Paul said, "Beware lest any man spoil you through philosophy and vain deceit, after the traditions of men, after the rudiments of the world, and not after Christ" (Col 2:8).

A critical danger to psychology is its grounding in humanist thinking, as was mentioned earlier. The Bible, for example, will teach that the human "heart is deceitful above all things and desperately wicked" (Jer. 17:9). Psychological counseling systems invented by atheists and agnostics will not guide an individual into biblical solutions as Scripture instructs, "Blessed is the man that walketh not in the counsel of the ungodly," (Psa. 1:1a). Reminders also come from other Scriptures, "Where is the wise? Where is the scribe? Where is the disputer of the world? Hath not God made foolish the wisdom of this world? For after that in the wisdom of God the world by wisdom knew not God, it pleased

---

[88] Thomas Szasz, *The Myth of Psychotherapy* (Syracuse, NY: Syracuse University Press, 1988), 67.

God by the foolishness of preaching to save them that believe" (1 Cor. 1:20). Psychology has entered the church, approved by the pastor, and is in vogue in all society. It has now gotten past the churches. The self-help section of the bookstore is bursting with new titles. As Gilley reveals, "[With] the invasion of psychology and its focus on felt needs ... the evangelical church has become a reflector of our times rather than a revealer."[89] So, human potential has entered the churches, liberal and conservative. Felt needs are one of the latest terms to be used for the psychologizing of the church.

Many counselors recommend that a reliable family support system be in place before the need arises, just as having a healthy support system as the need arises from PTSD is important. One psychologist relates this story:

> Patty, Susie, and Lisa dragged their husbands in for therapy. Each partner had gone to Iraq and Afghanistan believing in the wars ... each serviceman had become disillusioned overseas ... by the time each of these Iraq and Afghanistan veterans had been home less than a year, they were drinking bottles of hard liquor daily ... they were exhausted from nightmares and sleeplessness. Their families felt threatened by their rages, depression, and despair. Each was given large doses of medications to quell symptoms.[90]

---

[89] Gary Gilley, *This Little Church Went to Market* (Webster, NY: Evangelical Press, 2005), 48.

[90] Edward Tick, *Warriors Return* (Boulder, CO: Sounds True, 2014), 30.

Stories like this abound and go without an answer, while others seek help through military channels, which look similar. Hopelessness seems to be an end for many. Instances of family "secondary" PTSD has also plagued the home as a soldier returns from war. Soldiers attend classes about problems like these that may arise after deployment, but families are not usually briefed. Fear compounds problems when the victim fails to share the grief with family members and friends.

Tick describes multiple reasons for soldiers' survival through the accounts of soldiers as to how they escaped harm. Some attribute it to luck, while others say it is because they wore a certain amulet given to them from a family member or friend. God says, "There is no man that hath power over the spirit to retain the spirit; neither hath he power in the day of death: and there is no discharge in that war; neither shall wickedness deliver those that are given to it" (Eccl. 8:8). There are many alternatives of wickedness to choose from.

**Tribal rituals that know not God**

Tick describes a tribal ritual that a returning warrior takes as he is welcomed back to his village. He goes on to explain that many cultures give returning warriors certain rituals to perform to mark their return, and in so doing, they allow the warrior to come down from his experiences in battle, getting an understanding of the changes in environment he is entering. He is to remove the warrior's garb as well as the mind-set of war. He is not to bring the violence mind-set into the peace that exists when returning. Some soldiers choose to go the spiritual route through Christianity and seek out Jesus Christ as He is described as their Savior from sin to help them adjust. Complete pardon, complete peace, is promised: "Peace I leave with you, my peace I give unto you, not as the world giveth, give I unto you. Let not your heart be troubled, neither let it be afraid," (John 14:27).

## The Gospel

It is important to have established a personal relationship with Christ before the need due to PTSD arises. This is called preventive maintenance. Trouble will come; prepare for it now. Some soldiers who are sensitive to spirituality will avail themselves of prayer, Scripture reading, and attendance in religious services. Confusion lies for many in the thinking that religious service alone will make the difference. A religious service will last but for a short time, perhaps an hour. However, if one has a relationship with God, there is constant communion and communication and support to hold up the combatant. True Christianity is not a formal, step-by-step religious practice or an outline of a structured service displayed in a bulletin of a church handed out before a meeting. True Christianity and a right relationship with God are displayed in a daily experience of relationship with God in or out of a church service. Through prayer and Scripture, moment-by-moment assistance from God is available.

As the soldier gains a better understanding of God's complete control over all situations, the stress and trauma will subside. God in control brings peace to an individual. One way of describing the spiritual fruit of peace includes safety from any harm in a person's spirit and his body, which is produced only by the Spirit of God. If sin occurs, the soldier knows that they have forgiveness coming from an understanding and merciful God. As the Chaplain Corp pursues their role in providing spiritual care, they are challenged with another group- the spiritual.

One Pentagon Chief of Chaplain's office spokesman said soon after the approval of humanism, "the chaplaincy has generations ... (I)f they are spiritual, they may not consistently identify with one faith or one type of expression that seems to be the growing phenomenon ... we still ask how to support that audience."[91] The smorgasbord mentality of spirituality, where one might wish to take beliefs from several faiths and make his faith is often the style of today's spirituality. This does not happen only within the Protestant denominations. It is happening today through atheist/agnostics and freethinkers. Between Nordic, Wicca, and pagan-heathen groups. Individuals see these as an open source that is "outside the box" of what is seen otherwise as religious worship attendance. The idea of being religious may mean attending a worship service and seeing themselves performing a ritual as they go through the steps laid out in a bulletin. Jesus Christ directed his followers to be part of a local assembly that taught the Christian Scriptures, as He directed the writer of Hebrews to write: "not forsaking the assembling of ourselves together, as the manner of some is" (Heb. 10:25), recognizing that there are some who have left the assembly, just as He himself attended the Jewish synagogue in His day before the church was

---

91  Joe Gould, 19.

established. Jesus said that He would build His church (Matt. 16:18). He called Paul and others to go and establish new churches throughout their region at great personal cost.

The spiritual input of a local church should lead to a quality relationship with God and serve as group therapy during trauma rehabilitation. Hicks states, "The person who survives trauma the best is the one who has a preexisting quality relationship in his life."[92] Who better to have a quality relationship with than God through Jesus Christ? Noteworthy is the support system that is in place before trauma strikes. It will lend itself to helping the soldier through the trauma. There is no one better who can help than the God who created each one and knows him/her best. Few, however seem to be aware of prevention measures.

The Scriptures are replete with examples of people in need of a support system. God so often directly lends support. Abraham, when confronted with the command to sacrifice his son Isaac was ministered to by the Lord Himself when He stopped him from plunging the knife into his son and then provided a ram in his place (Gen. 22:1–14). "God tested Abraham (v.1), the writer quickly allays any doubt about God's real purpose. There is, then, no thought of an actual sacrifice of Isaac in the narrative, though in the mind of Abraham within the narrative that, of course that was the only thought that was entertained."[93] He saw it

---

92 Robert Hicks, *Failure to Scream* (Nashville: Thomas Nelson, 1993), 197.

93 John H. Sailhamer, "Genesis" in *Genesis, Exodus, Leviticus, Numbers*, vol. 2 of *The Expositors Bible Commentary*, ed. Frank E. Gaebelein (Grand Rapids: Zondervan, 1990), 167–168.

as an actual test because God had already told him that Isaac was to be the heir.

In another event, the Canaanite religion of Baal worship had permeated Israel's religious life. Elijah was determined to show Israel that this "god" that was so crucially connected to the weather would be outdone when Elijah prayed for what ended up being a three-year drought. "Given the lack of rain in specific seasons of the year in that region, Baal cultists had to explain why Baal could not guarantee rain at all times."[94] Then Elijah stepped up the challenge with a face-to-face competition with 450 prophets of Baal and another 400 grove prophets for back-up in what was a clash between God and backslidden Israel's false gods (Satan). God directed the steps concerning the sacrifice and gave Elijah great victory, (1 Kgs. 18:20–40). The fickle attitude of the people concerning the challenge Elijah presented to those who gathered to see the contest was revealed when no one spoke a word good or bad as to what they were about to see. Bible Commentator Paul House says, "Only Elijah and, ironically, the prophets of Baal have any conviction. Both Elijah and his counterparts believe their god to be the solution to Israel's problem."[95] Another example is when Moses confronts Pharaoh as Egypt experiences the ten plagues, and God intervenes each time on behalf of Moses, (Exo. 7:20—11:10). Moses needed to prove who Yahweh was to Pharaoh. Thus, a series of plagues struck Egypt, challenging the supposed dominance that that culture

---

94　Paul R. House, "1, 2, Kings." *In 1, 2 Kings.* Vol. 8 of the *New American Commentary* (Nashville: Broadman and Holman, 2003), 210–211.
95　House, 219.

claimed for their deities. "The suggestion is made that Pharaoh will request a wonderous deed as a vindication of the authority Moses and Aaron are claiming. Such a request may be implicit in Pharaoh's sarcastic question, 'Who is Yahweh?'"[96]

These are just a small sample of hundreds of similar accounts. The support needed by those written to in the Bible parallels in many ways those needs of the PTSD soldier and brings about a doctrinal foundation in the following ways. The Old Testament character King David was a man after God's own heart. During a Pauline address at his trial, he narrates a short form of Jewish history, bringing up the acts of David. Paul states that God had said of David that "I found David the son of Jesse, a man after my own heart" (Acts 13:22b). David wanted the same things God wanted but was also a man of war (1 Chr. 28:3). Many a military man that has experience in a war zone would struggle with a comparison of these two characteristics.

God must defend the good, defeating the bad, and in doing so, the blood of the enemy must be shed. A just war scenario is important. The Lord had kingdoms that needed to be subdued, and He chose David to do this work of bloodshed. David was able to go to God and express his sorrows of war through music, as was done through the Psalms, recognizing how God could minister in his life. David wrote after having experienced God's umbrella of protection: "I will love thee, O Lord, my strength. The Lord is my rock, and

---

96 John I. Durham, *Exodus,* vol. 3 of the *Word Biblical Commentary,* ed. Bruce M. Metzger (Waco, TX: Word Publishers, 1987.), 91.

my deliverer; my God, my strength, in whom I will trust; my buckler, and the horn of my salvation, and my high tower" (Psa. 18:1–2). Spurgeon quoted Joseph Caryl in *The Treasury of David*, when he wrote:

> It pleased holy David more that God was his strength than that he gave him strength; that God was his deliverer, than that he was delivered; that God was his fortress, his buckler, his horn, his high tower, than that he gave him the effect of all these. It pleased David, and it pleases all the saints more that God is their salvation. [97]

Men need a God who will hold them up in battle, rather than a God who must be held up. They carry a large-enough load through equipment and strain of mission and strains of home. America's soldiers are called upon to be shedders of blood when the time and cause is right. The Bible is written to those who need a protector, such as when soldiers are in combat zones around the world, and even to those who are just away from their homes. The soldier faces hardship and struggle in performing their duties. The biblical writers write about how suffering and hardship can be of God. Paul comforts the believer saying, "Blessed be God, even the Father of our Lord Jesus Christ, the Father of mercies, and the God of all comfort. Who comforteth us in all of our tribulation, that we may be able to comfort them which are in any trouble, by the comfort wherewith we ourselves are comforted of God" (2 Cor. 1:3–4). Gaebelein states:

---

97 Charles H. Spurgeon, *The Treasury of David* (Grand Rapids: Kregel, 1976), 78.

> Paul sees his suffering not merely as personally beneficial, driving him to trust God alone but also as directly benefitting those he ministered to … to experience God's comfort…in the midst of all one's affliction is to become indebted and equipped to communicate the divine comfort and sympathy to others who are in any kind of affliction or distress.[98]

The soldier needs to understand that God can make a difference in their healing and that prayer and the Bible can play a significant role in addressing these challenges.

Soldiers are driven to be physically fit and have regular programs to ensure that this fitness happens and that this training takes place according to Army Field Manual FM 21–20. This is done to ensure that when the physical strain of battle occurs, the soldier can endure. The soldiers receive resiliency training as stated in the CSF2 (Comprehensive Soldier and Family Fitness) manual. This spiritual training addresses the mind and the human spirit (which is dead apart from God) and is intended to be another training and prevention tool to the combat soldier. An injury can take place in the mind and soul of a soldier when he witnesses, for example, a fellow soldier killed or injured or he himself is physically injured. It is at this point the soldier needs to have a spiritual resiliency reserve he can draw upon to expedite healing. Sometimes it is nothing more than getting a question satisfactorily answered concerning death and dying.

---

98  Gaebelein, *Vol 10,* 320.

Jesus taught resiliency when He trained His disciples about the house built upon a rock (Matt. 7:24). When the traumas of life hit, the house of the person's life, the house was able to stand because of the moral foundation of the rock (Jesus). Unfortunately, today the rock of resiliency as taught within the military is not Christ but is found within oneself. Man, believing himself to be the center of all things has the answers, having the answers man proclaimed himself wise, thus he becomes the fool (Roman 1:22).

As mentioned earlier, man as god is taught in eastern New Age philosophy. God, in Romans, states, "So then they that are in the flesh cannot please God" (Rom. 8:8). When a man does not follow God's directions, man does things his own way, pleasing himself. With this philosophy, the military logically yet unknowingly is consenting to the need by offering humanism as a religious preference. Humanism has come out of the shadows and now is on full display as a person's mainstay for resiliency. When replacing God's Word, "the darkness created because of this leads to a desire for spiritual encounters (experiences)."[99] This is where the New Age Movement from eastern religions moves in and attempts to fill the void.

Much of what is New Age comes from the East. Practices such as yoga (what used to be Transcendental Meditation) are Hindu prayer exercises and are familiar to those who recommend various exercises coupled with prescribed medications. McMahon explains:

---

99  Roger Oakland, *Faith Undone* (Silverton, OR: Lighthouse Trails Pub, 2007), 50.

Yoga is a Sanskrit word that means 'yoking' and refers to union with Braham ... The goal of yoga is 'self-realization,' to realize the atman, the individual soul, is identical with Braham, the universal soul, i.e., that you and god are one; indeed, that you are god but just don't know it and need, through yoga, to discover this great truth.[100]

---

100  T. A. McMahon, The Berean Call, "The Avatar Gospel—A Newsletter Classic," June 8, 2018. Accessed 9 Jun 2018.

# CHAPTER 8

## Is Today's Psychology the Best Way?

In recent years, with further research, there has been an updating and revising of the descriptive terms concerning PTSD. For many, there has been an ethical or moral injury that has occurred. The evolving of terms concerning PTSD is now about removing the idea of a disorder. Removing the disorder has helped some. For others, the concern is for a violation of a personal ethical code. Moral Injury has been the latest way in addressing spiritual aspects of PTSD.

Moral injury connotes a wounding of the conscience to the extent that shame and guilt are a significant factor due to a violation of a personal standard. This personal standard violation fits naturally into the contemporary view of postmodernism in that for the individual there is a personal subjective morality. PTSD therapies that include Exposure Therapy (EP) have shown to help somewhat—temporarily. The idea here is to expose the trauma, letting the individual talk about it with others that have experienced similar trauma. Some believe this exposure will bring to remembrance traumatic events in a controlled environment instead of experiencing the intrusive nightmare, daydream, or other dissociative episodes. The intent with EP is to seek forgiveness from the situation, and thus forgetfulness where the event will no longer intrude. Grimsley observes, "The theoretical model, however, does conclude with a component of forgetfulness. After one remembers, one can choose to forget, because one has first addressed the traumatic memory. Remembering and forgiving are in the past tense ... one must remember to forget and one must remember to forgive."[101]

An important component that one must be made aware of is who has been wronged and from whom one receives forgiveness. God promises to forgive all sin once the individual has a personal relationship with God through the Lord Jesus Christ. God can forgive all sins, both those realized and those that are not known but shown to the sinner. The National Center for Posttraumatic Stress Disorder has said that people will try to get around reminders of the trauma they experienced. This idea works only for a short time. Prolonged Exposure Therapy (PET) helps those hurting face their fears. It has the intended goal of giving them more control of their lives. (We spoke earlier of the importance of control in our lives), but who should have ultimate control? To whom does one take their problems? Would not one who is troubled do better by giving over the control of their trauma to God?

To many around the world, God controlling one's circumstances becomes a relative term, and the control

---

101 Charles W. Grimsley, *PTSD and Moral Injury: The Journey to Healing through Forgiveness.* (Eatonville, FL: Xulon Press, 2017), 21.

one experiences within their own life in America is much different from other cultures around the world. Time does not heal all wounds; it makes them worse. How one remembers makes a difference in what truly needs healing. God can make that difference if He is in control of one's life. An individual may feel that they have full cognizance of those things that trouble him/her. God can make up the difference in one's faulty memory and can bring complete healing. Grimsley explains, "Authentic forgiveness is an actionable dynamic and can only happen when a person remembers the injustice and chooses to forgive and move forward."[102] The apostle Paul told the Philippians in Phil 3:13b-14 '…forgetting those things which are behind, and reaching forth into those that are before, I press toward the mark of the prize of the high calling of God in Christ Jesus." If one does not have a goal or prize of reaching toward the things that God has for them, they would be left with nothing but those past sad, frustrating, and burdening experiences.

Each person has a separate moral base of ethics. America's relativistic culture makes the moral injury label a more palatable foundation from which to work. Since each person can make up their own personal ethical standard, "moral injury is the pain that is the result of damage to the combat veteran's own moral foundation … the leading symptom of moral injury is a violation of what one considers wrong."[103] The moral injury view differs from PTSD because PTSD majors on various forms of fear. When these fears take charge,

---

102   Grimsley, 27.
103   Grimsley, 204.

they can cause severe distress, depression, and even for some, suicide. Moral injury exposure results in grief, loss, and shame.

**God's Way**

Man must come to realize that within each person is a nature separated from God by sin. In Romans 7, Paul explains man's trauma when sin entered into human nature. The eighth verse explains that without a law (moral standard), sin was dead. Verse 9 continues with "for I was alive without the law once: but when the commandment came, sin revived, and I died" (Rom. 7:9). Man has developed, through pride, his own moral standard. Man's standard never rises to God's moral standard. The problem coming within moral injury is man's standard has superseded God's standard, and in the process, man has put upon himself an unnecessary standard. When Christ died on the cross, He was allowing man the opportunity not only to receive this new standard but the power to follow it. No psychologist nor medical doctor, nor even an ordained minister, no matter how professional or how many years of practice can give a man or woman the ability to follow the perfect standard that Christ freely offers.

Paul, in Romans 7, continues in explaining the frustration that lies in trying to achieve a personal moral standard apart from God. In Romans 7:15, Paul states, "For that which I do allow (understand) not: for what I would that do I not; but what I hate, that do I. If then I do that which I would not, I consent unto the law that it is good." Later in verses 19 and 20, Paul continues, "for the good that I would I do not: but the evil which I would not, that I do. Now if I do that I would not, it is more I that do it, but sin that dwelleth in me." In paraphrasing the next verse, it might state, "I find then a law (moral standard), when I would do good (obey personally questionable orders), evil is present with me. How is one to solve this moral dilemma?" In the next verse, 22, Paul states: "For I delight in the law of God after the inward man."

Christ obeys the law of God, and that righteousness is passed onto the believing sinner at salvation, fulfilling the required righteousness demanded by the law. The sinner obtains God's requirement for perfection in Christ's righteousness given to all who trust Christ for salvation and full forgiveness, as explained by "For what the law could not do, in that it was weak through the flesh, God sending his own Son in the likeness of sinful flesh, and for sin, condemned sin in the flesh: that the righteousness of the law might be fulfilled in us, who walk not after the flesh, but after the Spirit" (Rom. 8:3–4).

John Phillips comments, "Deliverance from the control of sin could never come through our own efforts to the Mosaic law … It was not that God asked too much of man, for He can be satisfied with nothing less than absolute perfection. It was that man in the flesh simply could not live up to the claims of God's law."[104] God cannot arbitrarily hand out forgiveness. Christ made the payment on the cross. Furthermore, Dunn states, "Weakness is not a term of accusation or

---

104 John Phillips, *Exploring Romans: An Expository Commentary* (Grand Rapids: Kregel, 1969), 123.

condemnation in Paul; it is simply descriptive of the human condition."[105] Verse 23 further explains the frustration that arises when a man sets his own moral standard and fails to live up to it. Paul reminds, "But I see another law in my members, warring against the law of my mind, and bringing me into captivity to the law of sin which is in my members (flesh)," (Rom. 7:23). The only way out of this moral injury dilemma is through Jesus Christ, as Paul explains in the last verses of chapter 7: "O wretched man that I am who shall deliver me from the body of this death. I thank God through Jesus Christ our Lord. So then with the mind I serve the law of God; but with the flesh the law of sin" (Rom. 7:24–25). One who decides for themselves that their personal moral standard is suitable needs to rethink and consider what the Bible says in Romans 10:3. "For they being ignorant of God's righteousness, and going about to establish their own righteousness, have not submitted themselves unto the righteousness of God." One day their fear will come to ahead and they will face God with their guilt on judgment day. A person's guilt of sin, and their fear of judgment can be permanently removed with Christ's forgiveness. Christ paid for it all.

One should wish to increase personal knowledge of the biblical PTSD recovery methods topic and thereby assist PTSD sufferers or those closely related, either relational or professional, in recovery. In all that is done, the Word of God is to be the central tool. It is to be the basis for all study. With that in consideration,

---

105 James D.G. Dunn, *Word Biblical Commentary Romans 1–8* (Dallas: Word Publishing, 1988), 420–421.

it is my desire assist soldiers and others to find non-psychology and drug-free answers to PTSD. God has set the parameters that He would want from a student of the Word, as far as life-changing decisions and a new life lived for Christ is concerned. There is a strong witness to the effectiveness of the Word of God, whereas the postmodernist rejects absolutes.

Rejecting absolutes diminishes the role God plays in a person's life if there is no belief in God and makes all things negotiable. "If there are no absolutes in the objective realm, neither can there be absolutes in the subjective realm ... postmodernism is passive, cynical, and insecure."[106] Assisting other professionals in coming to a belief in Christ because of the salvation and healing of PTSD would be a significant professional goal, as relativism taught through the mental health professionals brings about temporary solutions at best.

**Which god makes the difference?**

Concerns should be voiced, expressing unease about the ability of a wounded spirit to recognize their spiritual need and rather than apply the psychological and medical help, to choose instead a spiritual route in obtaining the cure from PTSD and moral injury. In getting help from God, the soldier must first "believe that he [*God*] is and that he is a rewarder of them that diligently seek him" (Heb 11:6b). That is the path of faith. Dokoupil of *Newsweek* says, "Despite three decades of research and billions of dollars in government funding,

---

106 Gene Edward Veith, Jr., *Postmodern Times; A Christian Guide to Contemporary Thought and Culture* (Wheaton: Crossway, 1994), 83.

The health of America's servicemen and women are not getting better, they are getting worse, overall. Self-harm is now the leading cause of death for members of the Army, which has seen its suicide rate double since 2004."[107] Researchers have studied the trauma issues of the contemporary warrior and have concluded that there is something different in the trauma issues of America's contemporary veteran. These soldiers have grown up in a culture of postmodernism that precludes any need for spiritual faith in a God once embraced by their forefathers, a Christian faith that was held in some fashion, giving the individual some style of faith. However, somewhere they have been detached from this previously held ethic and replaced it by relativistic values and what some have termed practical atheism or eastern mysticism, which is a driving force in much of the medical practitioners.

Charnock explains, "Shame put a bar to the first, and natural reason to the second; yet, perhaps, he had sometimes some doubts, whether there were a God or no. He wished there were not any, and sometimes hoped there were none at all."[108] The godlessness within medicine when it comes to studying a simple strand of DNA is hard to explain. Christian counselor and author Davis Powlison adds to the discussion with an interesting thought states, "the fatal flaw in both research psychology and the personality theories [is] that [they] cannot explain why people do what they do because they exclude the truth a priori and elevate

---

107 Dokoupil, T http://www.newsweek.com/new-theory-ptsd-and-veterans-moral-injury. Accessed 8 Aug, 2018.
108 Stephen Charnock, *On Practical Atheism* 1864–1866, 24, Kindle.

secondary factors to primary significance."[109] Keeping the important things, a priority must be done through having the mind of Christ. Granted, there are many ideas that fight for first place in a person's thinking, so it is crucial that in order to have a quieted spirit and soul the key is to give one's self over to the Lord. The Lord Jesus states, "Come unto me, all ye that labour and are heavy laden, and I will give you rest" (Matt 11:28). Nouthetic counselor Jim Berg comments, "Any attempt to solve life's problems apart from Jesus Christ will result in failure."[110] Any problem can be solved with Christ, unfortunately many in America are not of that mindset.

What would have been considered solutions within the Christian community concerning PTSD in the realm of Christian psychology, when examined biblically, are not seen as the Christian solution. This writer will review both humanistic psychology and what is termed "Christian psychology." Adams explains that "From the beginning, human change depended upon counseling. Man was created as a being whose very existence is derived from and dependent upon a Creator whom he acknowledged as such and from whom he must obtain wisdom and knowledge through revelation ... even before the fall."[111] Man was made in

---

109 David G Myers, Stanton L. Jones, Robert C. Roberts, Paul J. Watson, John H. Coe, Todd W. Hall, Davis Powlison, *Psychology and Christianity. Five Views,* Eric L. Johnson ed. (Downers Grover, IL IVP Academic, 2010), 144.
110 Jim Berg, *Taking Time to Quiet Your Soul* (Greenville, SC: JourneyForth Books, 2005), 62.
111 Jay E. Adams, *A Theology of Christian Counseling* (Grand Rapids: Zondervan, 1979), 1.

God's image and having been made in that condition, man has a need to be directly in contact with God's plan and His purpose; otherwise, there is an incompleteness that exists within man in which he is searching for. Adams continues, "Any attempt to transform him into an autonomous being not only constitutes rebellion against the creator, but is bound to fail ... from the fall onward has been the root of the bitter fruit of chaos and misery."[112]

Counseling, be it psychological, integrational, Christian psychology, transformational psychology, or biblical psychology, has developed and brought many theories together and sometimes into conflict with one another. "Yet Christian interest in psychology has exploded over the last fifty years. Countless books have been written by Christians that describe our personalities, our boundaries, our dysfunctional development, our relationships, and their problems."[113]

## Pseudo-Psychologies

Secular psychologists like Schiraldi, Tick, Matsakis, and Shay; Christian psychologists such as Narramore, Hicks, Crabb, Dobson, and Collins; as opposed to Nouthetic counselors, counting Adams, Anderson, Bobgan, Lambert, and Powlison, and so forth, will be discussed within the framework of the theoretical due to the first group downplaying biblical principles and the nouthetic counselors backing the Bible. When it comes to helping those with spiritual issues, they will give credence to a spiritual piece of the human being,

---

112  Adams, 2.
113  Myers, 9.

but some authors, at times, will tend to steer toward and provide the lion share of their time and energy to the psychological aspects of the issue. In 1960, Clyde Narramore wrote *The Psychology of Counseling*, and in 1966, Narramore wrote *Encyclopedia of Psychological Problems*. In the latter, he is quick to point out the great and marvelous discoveries found within psychology and its popularity within the society at large. He adds the spiritual dimension, speaking of how man "does not receive the things of the Spirit of God: for they are foolishness unto him: neither can he know them for they are spiritually discerned" (1 Cor. 2:14). However, from there, he leaves off further biblical solutions.

With a cursory look through the book, one can see a pattern of keying on the psychological aspects of the issues people face with long passages but giving short mention or no mention of a Bible answer. In covering anxiety, Clyde Narramore, Christian psychologist, in giving an example that gives place to the Bible but leaving the patient with the idea that the counselor is the savior, states "Spiritual growth is an important factor in overcoming anxiety ... Such spiritual concepts, however, are not gained automatically from a lecture. Instead, they are usually developed over a period of time as a client identifies himself closely with a dedicated believer (counselor)."[114] Christ, the difference maker, is not mentioned in the discussion, but rather the counselor becomes the difference maker. This is part of the process bringing together psychology with Scripture, with psychology taking the leading

---

114 Clyde M. Narramore, *Encyclopedia of Psychological Problems* (Grand Rapids, MI: Zondervan, 1966), 42–43.

role. It "demeaned the role of pastors, supposedly limited to Scripture in the understanding of the human condition."[115] This movement toward limiting ministers to so-called spiritual matters and readdressing other issues as psychological, requiring specialized training, adapts new humanistic psychology measures, replacing biblical advice. Bobgan continues when he states that the dilemma began back when

> ... the soul has been reduced to mind, the mind has been confused with the brain, and the church has relegated mental-emotional distress and problems of living to professional practitioners who specialize in the mind 'sciences.' Separating the mind from the spirit leads to the erroneous conclusions that the Bible is incapable of dealing with problems of thinking and behaving. Both the psychological way and the spiritual way provide nonscientific solutions to mental-emotional-behavioral problems. The spiritual way provides biblical solutions; the psychological way provides man-made solutions.[116]

The writer of Hebrews plainly states, "The Word of God is quick and powerful, and sharper than any two-edged sword, piercing even to the dividing asunder of soul and spirit, and of the joints and marrow" (Heb 4:12a). David says that his "delight is in the law of the

---

115 Martin Bobgan, *PsychoHeresy* (Santa Barbara, CA: EastGate Publishers, 2012), 275.

116 Bobgan, *How to Counsel from Scripture.* (Chicago: Moody Press, 1985), 12–13.

Lord and in his law doth he meditate day and night" (Psa. 1:2). The Bible should be the source to which any believer goes. Further, putting the most important information upfront would be better for some who will investigate.

"Low self-esteem is popular because it is much easier to accept the idea of having low self-esteem than confessing evil, ungodly, self-centered thoughts, and then repenting through believing what God has said in his Word."[117] Dobson also says in his book *Hide or Seek*, "Thus, if inadequacy and inferiority are so universally prevalent at all ages of life at this time, We must ask ourselves 'why?'"[118] Bobgan says it best, answering, "He evidently subscribes to Adler's theories of the universality of inferiority feelings."[119] "Gary Collins, a licensed clinical psychologist, has written extensively in the promotion of integrating psychotherapy into Christianity."[120] A troubling statement occurs in Collins's book, *A Biblical Basis for Christian Counseling for People Helpers*, where he writes, "Most counselors look for methods that are effective and practical for bringing changes in people's lives. We may realize that some of these therapeutic techniques built on philosophical presuppositions that are *not consistent with what the Bible teaches,* but we feel confident in our ability to use each method without accepting its

---

117 Bobgan, *PsychoHeresy*, 279.
118 James Dobson, *Hide and Seek* (Old Tappan, NJ: Fleming R. Revell, 1979), 17.
119 Bobgan, *Prophets of PsychoHeresy II*, 99.
120 Bobgan, *PsychoHeresy*, 284.

underlying philosophy"[121] [emphasis added]. The author goes on to say that as long as the practitioner is aware of the dangers, we can apply humanistic tricks successfully. Perhaps Collins and others should research the origins of psychology. Anderson suggests, "While favoring this approach's emphasis on the authority and importance of Scripture, Crabb disagrees with the orientation because he views it as too narrow."[122] The same could be said about yoga. For many, yoga seems to be a cure for many physical and mental troubles. Even some Christians use yoga. God says in the Bible that we are not to be a part of the unfruitful works of darkness. Understanding yoga and what is intended in its origins would cause many to reexamine the practice and realize its dangers. Yoga, as taught by the Yogi Bhajan, says, "You can know the Unknown and see the Unseen. If you spend two hours per day in meditation, God will meditate on you the rest of the day ... Indeed, the purpose is to achieve the realization that each individual practicing yoga is god."[123] Hunt joins in the chorus of cautions against yoga stating that "the ancient yogis warned of the dangers that yoga posed to practitioners, declaring that one's guru must always be present during the 'awakening' that yoga was designed to produce."[124]

Even more recently, other counselors who have a concern for a biblical approach to counseling and do not address the specifics of PTSD but address the

---

121 Gary R. Collins, *The Biblical Basis of Christian Counseling for People Helping* (Colorado Springs: Navpress, 2001), 14.
122 Neil T. Anderson, Terry E. Zuehlke and Julianne S. Zuehlke, *Christ Centered Therapy* (Grand Rapids: Zondervan, 2000), 66.
123 Hunt. *Yoga and the Body of Christ,* 2, Kindle.
124 Hunt, 44.

same manuals that psychology references, have looked into the Diagnostic and Statistical Manual (DSM). Lambert warns, "For biblical counselors, the DSM paints an inadequate and misleading picture. It fails to express, recognize, or understand the spiritual aspect of problem that afflict people."[125]

Biblical instruction as well as implementation is essential. Wayne Mack discusses the importance of giving pertinent biblical instruction and ensuring the importance of the teaching part of the counselee's life. Mack states, "Biblical counseling seeks to promote holiness or *biblical change* as a life-style. It endeavors to foster the implementation and integration of biblical principles into people's lives so they will become *consistently Christ centered and Christ-like in every area of life including their desires, thought, attitudes, feelings, behavior*"[126] [emphasis in original].

Throughout His Word, God has expressed his concern for those who are in distress. God promises an answer that will fit into any life, and when applied to a willing patient, answers will come and manifest themselves as truly workable; allowing God to take charge completely and in all circumstances, for it is in Him that real hope lies. Curington points out, "If you will live with a conscious effort to obey these two responsibilities, the first will remove your addiction, and the second will keep it from coming back. "*Jesus said unto him, thou shalt love the Lord thy God with all thy heart (or, your emotions), and with all thy soul (or, your will).*

---

125 Heath Lambert, *A Theology of Biblical Counseling* (Grand Rapids: Zondervan, 2016), 323.

126 John F. MacArthur, Jr and Wayne Mack, *Introduction to Biblical Counseling: A Basic Guide to the Principles and Practice of Counseling* (Dallas: Word Pub, 1994), 284.

*And with all your mind (or, your thoughts. This is the first and great commandment"* [127] (Matt. 22:37–38) [italics in original]. Scripture contains the solace and strength that a PTSD sufferer needs. Man struggles with giving up control due to alienation with his Creator. Man's sin has separated him from his God, and he distrusts Him to bring about solutions. God has one's best interest in His mind as Jeremiah writes, "For I know the thoughts that I think toward you, saith the LORD, thoughts of peace, and not of evil, to give you an expected end." (Jer. 29:11). "An implied contrast [is] between the certainty of God, and the vain imaginations in which the Jews indulged themselves ... for they were wont absurdly to measure God by their own ideas."[128] These ideas will include all the things that plague a person with PTSD: guilt, lack of peace, fear, broken relationships, and all the habits that developed in an attempt to solve or put out of one's mind those things that are unrelenting to a wounded spirit.

Exploring the plethora of resources that are available on all sides of the spectrum of PTSD, I a key resource of literature must include the book *Wounded Spirits.*[129] Diagnosis and treatment makes a big difference in outcomes. The seminal Bible verse I use is: "The spirit of a man will sustain his infirmity; but a wounded spirit who can bear?" (Prov. 18:14). "A man sustains the life of his body, and the trials of life, by the strength and

---

127 Steve Curington, *Nevertheless I Live* (Rockford, Il: Steven Boyd Pub, 2004), 39.
128 John Calvin, "Jeremiah," *Jeremiah and Lamentations,* vol. XI of the *Calvin Commentary,* ed. John Owen (Grand Rapids: Baker Book, 1998), 431.
129 Carragher.

the energy of his mind. But if the mind be wounded, if this be cast down, if slow consuming care and grief have shot the dagger into the soul, what can sustain the man? Nothing but the unseen God."[130] It is not a wounded body, or a wounded brain, known in the psychology profession as traumatic brain injury, or TBI. When a warrior experiences a wounded spirit, then the ability to overcome stress or trauma-producing events are hard to overcome. God must be the central part of this recovery. It is further noted by Allen P. Ross, the word *crushed* can replace *wounded,* as seen in his commentary. Ross observes, "A healthy spirit brings a healing to the body. This is affirmed by contrasting a healthy spirit with a crushed spirit: a healthy attitude sustains a person but depression is unbearable."[131] This may be the reason for a high suicide rate among those affected by PTSD.

The main traumatic event occurs at conception, and the sin nature is at this point embedded in the human soul. This one event, when a sinner is conceived in a womb, is the beginning of the trauma. A person will live their life in sin unless at some time in the person's life after God shows them their need for salvation, they choose to have God regenerate their spirit so that it may begin communication with God's Holy Spirit. Otherwise, they will fail to receive the instruction that they so desperately need to make the right choices

---

130 Adam Clarke, "Proverbs," in *Job- Song of Solomon,* vol. III *Clarke's Commentary* (Nashville: Abingdon), 753.

131 Allen P. Ross, "Proverbs," in *Psalms, Proverbs, Ecclesiastes, Song of Solomon,* Vol. 5 of *The Expository Bible Commentary,* ed. Frank E. Gaebelein (Grand Rapids: Zondervan, 1991), 1026.

at critical times and go in God's direction. For an individual to be set free from the power of addictions and other sins in their life, they must understand that there is only one way that this will happen. Jesus speaking to those that believed on him, "If ye continue in my word, then ye are my disciples indeed; and ye shall know the truth, and the truth shall make you free" (John 8:31b–32). Hastings comments, "Truth is the expression of reality, a statement in harmony with fact."[132]

Jesus continued to explain to the group he was speaking to that he was referring to being made free from sin. Many believe that sin is a choice. One can choose right or not choose right. The sin nature is present, and because of its presence, Jeremiah gives the reader something else to consider: "The heart is deceitful above all things, and desperately wicked: who can know it?" (Jer. 17:9). The sin nature in every human being is what controls a person in their thinking and actions. The heart is deceitful (lies); it is desperately (furiously, with rage) wicked.

Man needs to have this vital information, which is overlooked by psychology—the need to be born-again. Man is seemingly capable of doing good only because he is made in the image of God, but with that image comes a sin-marred condition. An individual does not desire proper instruction unless the Spirit of God is living in him. Only the power of God can overtake most problems. Even if a person can overcome

---

[132] James Hastings, John vol. 1 ed. The Speakers Bible, *The Gospel According to John Vol 1* (Grand Rapids: Baker Books, 1962), 191.

addictions on his own, that "good work" of overcoming those habits will not bring him into the presence of God in heaven one day. Only salvation through Christ can accomplish this. Overcoming an addiction in this life is commendable wherein some are able to obtain, but it is for this life only.

Psychology as a field was expanded under Sigmund Freud and came into its own in the mid- and late-1800s. In the twentieth century, Freud tried developing a dovetail effect with psychoneurosis. When considering psychology and psychoneurosis, "Both theories centered on how the psyche needed to defend itself from its own inner forces in order to maintain a kind inner stability. But he had still been unable to precisely define those forces that disrupted the mind."[133] Psychology at its base lacks a godly influence. Freud was a secular Jew. Early in his life, he examined the place that religion or God might have in man's thinking. He decided that belief in the Bible must be removed. Thomas Szasz has this to add: "It is clear from his [*Freud's*] report that leaving Vienna for Paris, Freud has decided to give up the study of real disease and the practice of real medicine and embark on the study of fake diseases and the practice of fake medicine."[134] When Freud spoke on religious terms, he would warn others of how unreliable the Bible was, and "Freud reduced religious beliefs to illusion."[135] He also saw religion as evil and a place of mental issues. Author

---

133 George Makari, *Revolution in Mind* (New York: Harper Collins, 2008), 85.
134 Thomas Szasz, *Psychiatry: The Science of Lies* (Syracuse, NY: University Press, 2008), 286. Kindle.
135 Bobgan, *PsychoHeresy,* 132.

Martin Bobgan believed that "Religious bias colored the psychological systems of both Freud and Jung. "They were not dealing with science, but with beliefs, values, attitudes, and behavior. Because they were working in areas in which the Bible gives the authoritative words of God they were developing antibiblical religions."[136]

Symptoms of PTSD will be examined according to psychological foundations and the biblically Christian (theological) foundations. The examination will be made as to why they occur according to these differing views. Then cures from each side will be examined. Due to the number of symptoms of PTSD (200-plus) and space available in this book. Fear, guilt, anger, nightmares, flashbacks, avoidance (isolation), moral injury, in addition to the topic of pain and suffering, are examined. When examining psychology, it is vital to consider the background of Freud.

Freud has an interesting past:

> Consider also when one examines the background of psychology's founders, "Freud was a cocaine addict and lusted after his own mother. Jung was suicidal and communed with a demon. Rogers abandoned his cancer stricken, dying wife for another woman but relieved his guilt by allegedly contacting his deceased wife spirit through a Ouija board. Rogers later ended his own life through assisted suicide.[137]

---

136 Ibid., 132.
137 Dave Hunt, *Psychology and the Church* (Bend, OR: Berean Call, 2008), 21, 22.

These are important items when examining the various procedures that involve psychology. The foundational philosophy behind his ideas must be examined.

The military is tapping into many resources to help the soldier recover from whatever injuries he/she has incurred. Along with the continuing medical research in exploring the brain and supposed associated mental faculties, in their attempt to aid the soldier with mental trauma, programs have developed through various organizations that offer retreats, cruises, and even hunting trips. Other programs, such as karate instruction, meditation, and yoga, have been included as an aid to soldiers and families that face post-deployment adjustments.[138] These are all considered temporary pain or symptom relief measures. They show care and concern, but they have not proven to cure.

For as much as those in the profession of health and mental health care show concern, they attempt to treat using the latest and the perceived greatest means. However, "The gospel is still the power of God unto salvation, but it has been rejected out of hand by many because PTSD is not viewed as a spiritual issue. The mental health community thinks new ideas are needed, apparently, and new methods to reach the hurting. The religious community desires new techniques to promote the church, "… people, we were told were not rejecting the gospel message or Christ; they were rejecting our out-of-date … philosophy."[139] The increasing secular mind-set of the society-at-large

---

138 Blog.wired.com/defense/2008/10/samurai-soldiers.html, troops use Samurai meditation to soothe PTSD.

139 Gary Gilley, *This Little Church Went to Market* (Webster, NY: Evangelical Press, 2005), 16.

and in the military environment today creates within its ranks a growing relativistic practice. London claims, "When the advocates of secularism claim to be in opposition to religion, they ought to be reminded that, despite protests to the contrary, they speak for and represent a religion of the head and the heart. What they lack is a religion of the soul."[140]

The purpose of spiritual recovery through the study of the Bible will be to give soldiers an understanding that pain is a real and necessary part of the maturing process, and one needs not to avoid suffering under the direction of a loving and sovereign God. The individual must recognize God, who knows just what is required to grow as the one who can place the right amount of stress on you to bring about a continuing process of maturation. At the same time, the soldiers can pick up skills that will be helpful to others when the soldier's comrades in arms go through their difficult times. As PTSD sufferers learn to deal with their traumatic issues, they are then encouraged to use what they have learned not only in their lives but also to help others with their problems. Paul proclaims, God "Who, comforteth us in all our tribulation, that we may be able to comfort them which are in any trouble, by the comfort wherewith we ourselves are comforted of God" (2 Cor. 1:4). Charles Stanley concurs and adds, "We discover things about ourselves in the deepest, darkest valley experiences. We discover how much real courage we have. We discover the degree of our faith. We discover the focus of our faith."[141]

---

140 Herbert London, *America's Secular Challenge* (NY: Brief Encounters, 2008), 22.
141 Charles Stanley, *God Is in Control* (Nashville: Thomas Nelson, 2003), 44 Kindle.

A proper theological foundation must include the Bible. The Bible teaches healing not only of the body but also of the soul (mind, will, and emotions) and spirit. These areas are connected and function together. Below, the theological foundation and the theoretical foundation are compared to show the strict differences between the two. The Bible has the answers to these issues, and unfortunately, the medical and mental health communities are not willing to explore the biblical options for those who are hurting with PTSD. Grogan, however, expounds, "Compliance with this instruction is therapeutic; it will be health to the body and nourishment for the frame."[142]

The crucial aspect of morality is its source. In Christianity, the source of morality is God—and not in anything arbitrary. Other belief systems have a source of morality that is subjective, based on a person's experience. "[*A morality that can function consistently*] is rooted in his eternal goodness. Nor does it seem to us to be arbitrary, because it meshes with the way we have been put together ... in the deep structure of our own created conscience."[143] Paul, the apostle, said that this vital information concerning God's truth is written in the heart. It can be held down and suppressed, even ignored, but it cannot be removed. With the current trends in postmodern thought, relativism brings about less interest in specific religious views. "Relativism

---

142 Geoffrey W. Grogan, "Isaiah" in *Isaiah—Ezekiel* vol.6 of *The Expositors Bible Commentary*, ed. Frank E. Gaebelein (Grand Rapids: Zondervan, 2008), 65.

143 Paul Copan, Scott B. Luley, and Stan W. Wallace ed. *Philosophy: Christian Perspectives for the New Millenium* (Addison, TX, Norcross, GA: CLM/RZIM, 2003), 91.

denies ... the source of moral law is God, that the foundational moral principles are right for everyone, and denies that they are known to everyone."[144]

Postmodernism thought rejects absolutes. This diminishes the role God plays in one's life if there is a belief in God. This uncertainty about God makes all things negotiable. Veith says it this way: "If there are no absolutes in the objective realm, neither can there be absolutes in the subjective realm ... postmodernism is passive, cynical, and insecure."[145] When the proper theological foundation of God's Word is not present, chaos erupts within the soldier's soul.

The soldier wants to see the practical purpose of the Word of God in his healing. When events in combat bring up questions, such as "Why did I survive and someone else did not?" or "Could a loving God allow such atrocities?" a firm foundation of biblical truth can dispel any doubts. Society has attempted to eliminate God. When tragedy strikes, God suddenly returns to a person's conversation in words but generally with no authority and power. Many relegate morality to Sunday morning religion, but it is more than that if it is real. Adsit, adding to the thought, states, "We must never forget that Christianity is not supposed to be merely a religion or a philosophy of life, it is a relationship with a heavenly Father. In any relationship, there must be communication."[146]

---

[144] Copan, 92.

[145] Gene Edward Veith, Jr., *Postmodern Times: A Christian Guide to Contemporary Thought and Culture* (Wheaton: Crossway, 1994), 83.

[146] Chris Adsit, *The Combat Trauma Healing Manual: Christ-Centered Solutions for Combat Trauma* (Newport News: Military Ministry Press, 2007), 44.

According to Edward Tick in *Warriors Return,* "For veterans to come from psychiatry's reliance on medications that cannot quell spiritual strength anguish and moral pain ... It fails to come from religion's stock answers with assumptions of original sin and justifiable suffering."[147] God, on the other hand, says that man is incapable of helping himself. Mostly, there are glaring differences in how to solve the emotional issues of PTSD and the lingering effects of prescribed medication addictions that flow from mental health (behavioral health) and medical doctors, both military and civilian. Thinking they are helping, from this well-intended guidance of psychology and pharmaceuticals, an opioid epidemic has arisen and contributed to a growing suicide rate. "Opioids—prescription and illicit—are the primary driver of America's drug overdose deaths, according to Center for Disease Control. President Trump has called the opioid epidemic 'the worst drug crisis in American history.'"[148] Also, with well-intentioned advice, the patient is often left without hope, that is a never-ending reliance on the medicines and information resulting in no real answers. The opioid epidemic has come into greater focus with the president of the United States announcing that there is an opioid crisis occurring in the country.

Tick pronounces that leaders can do no wrong when they declare war, saying, "God chooses mortal rulers and that, as his chosen servants, they can do no wrong."[149] This is not to say that there were times

---

147 Edward Tick, *Warrior's Return: Restoring the Soul After War* (Boulder, CO: Sounds True, 2014), 200.
148 Joe Gould and David B Larter. In American Opioid Crisis, Military Lets Drug Shipments go by, Feb 15.
149 Tick, *War and the Soul,* 39.

when a ruler called for a just war. Tick connects war and religion. Tick states, "war has fostered religion, and religion war."[150] God and Lucifer fought the first war in heaven. Lucifer has seen to it since then that conflicts stemming from religion would continue. The difference in opinion continues over who should be worshiped and how worship should be conducted. Satan has no problem with a man finding religion in trying to solve PTSD so long as he does not find the true and only Savior, Jesus Christ, who can forgive sin, restore the soul to peace, and bring him home to heaven one day.

---

150  Tick, 270.

# Part II
# Compare and Contrast Theoretical and Theological Views

# CHAPTER 9

## Fear (Anxiety)

Marshall explains, "Fear is ever present, but it is uncontrolled fear that is the enemy of successful operation, and the control of fear depends upon the extent to which all dangers and distractions may be correctly anticipated and therefore understood."[151] With this backdrop for showing the way forward, consider the issues of PTSD. Fear, coupled with anxiety, is one of the greatest hindrances to a peaceful and calm life. Noah Webster describes it as "A painful emotion or passion excited by an expectation of evil, or the apprehension of impending danger."[152] Having a relationship with God, being connected, and in conversation with the Almighty, brings a greater quality of communication that is vital when all other things or persons deemed important are taken. Placing confidence in a buddy or spouse or even a therapist can be of great assistance,

---

151 S.L.A. Marshall, *The Problem of Battle Command in Future War* (New York: William Morrow and Company, 1947), 454 Kindle.
152 Noah Webster, *American Dictionary of the English Language* (San Francisco: Foundation for American Christian Education, 1828).

but there will be those times when all those resources are taken away or are simply not available. Fear in God himself otherwise it will eventually fail when we trust in others. It is key to whom then can one go? Says Robert Hicks:

> I would put in this category of important relationships our relationship with God … many of the issues inherent in the field of trauma studies have serious theological and spiritual significance. Also, the reader should have noted on the subject of heartiness that having meaning also pays a very important role as a predisposition factor. The person who has a genuine, vibrant, and realistic faith has a framework that can provide the needed meaning when no other meaning is found. Our faith can often make sense of the absurd.[153]

When one is genuine in their fear and faith that is already present, there is no need to scramble in trying to find something or someone else that will help. In doing so, there is the tendency to settle with the first thing that comes to them without close examination. One fears in what one relies on. Psychology and medications are what people fear (in other words, respect).

The theoretical response that emanates from psychology is man-centered and leans heavily upon self-help. Even when Christian psychologists attempt to bridge the gap between the Bible and psychology, when looking closely, the two cannot be one. Having

---

153 Robert Hicks, *Failure to Scream* (Nashville: Thomas Nelson, 1993), 198.

a fear in or respect for God will result in placing total faith in him and nothing else. In what appears to be an attempt to blur the lines of Bible and psychology, psychology tends to give credit to the counselor rather than to the Bible or God, thus decreasing faith.

Psychiatry and psychology tend to team up, looking for solutions to the issues of fear through medications. The American military lean heavily upon medications in order to keep the fighting force together for as long as possible to fight and win the wars the nation and its leaders call upon them to do. Here, locally in Fayetteville, outside of Ft. Bragg, NC, a Fox News Channel (FNC) report put significant light on the problem as Tucker Carlson reported on his prime-time television program. His report contained some startling information. The Veterans Administration has admitted to being complicit in the opioid epidemic among veterans. During the program, Public Broadcasting (PBS) was quoted in print that of those returning from Iraq and Afghanistan, nearly all received opioids for pain relief. According to the Center for Investigative Reporting seen on the same FNC show, there has been a 270 percent increase in opioid abuse in the last twelve years. Forty-seven percent abuse their medications, according to the *Wall Street Journal,* and FNC reports that there are no residential treatment facilities or detoxification facilities in the area. Also, there are only five doctors in the surrounding twenty-one counties that have any programs that dispense medications for overdose (OD) treatment. That statement is remarkable. Using medications to solve medication overdose is not the answer. FNC also stated that the veterans would stay hooked until they OD or go to a private clinic in nearby Fayetteville to receive methadone, which sees hundreds daily. Another PBS source was quoted by Carlson that "Vets are two times more likely to OD than non-vets."[154] Much of the pain relievers taken by our military for "pain" may actually be a misdiagnosis of the soul's symptom of fear. The intermingled practice of pharmacology and psychology has been around for a while. This relationship "which allowed business interests to determine how doctors should think, and whom and what they should treat, shaped not only the practice of medicine but eventually also the practice of psychology, for it is from within medicine that the current practice of the Psychology Industry emerged."[155]

Fear can manifest itself in many forms and can therefore receive many styles of treatments. A rapidly popularized remedy is a holistic approach of Eastern religious practices namely: massage, acupuncture, meditation, and yoga. These four were options brought out in that low-attended meeting I mentioned above. Also, given increasing visibility is yoga. These practices have the potential, according to recent occult studies, to open an individual to demonic activity, much like the drugs that were introduced into the culture in the 1960s where veterans and others went to in an attempt to find answers. "Philip St Romain, a substance abuse counselor and devout Catholic lay minister began his journey while practicing contemplative prayer ... not [*through*] zen, not yoga, but a Christian form of

---

154 *Drugs,* Tucker Carlson. Fox News Channel, April 12, 2017.
155 Tana Dineen, *Manufacturing Victims* (New York: Robert Davies Multimedia, 2000), 240.

these practices."156 Meditation, if the mind is focused wrongly, can also be dangerous.

> Psychiatrists are dealing with the possibility of a medication that can counter PTSD disorders, those that have come from the battlefield and are unable to sleep because of all of the trauma and so on, but the fear of the discussion committees is this, if we are to find a drug that is so able to erase the memory of horrific things to what end would that drug be put to a rapist, or a mass murderer who the morning after a series of crimes can just swallow the pill and not feel any sense of guilt whatsoever.157

This relationship "which allowed business interests to determine how doctors should think, and whom and what they should treat, shaped not only the practice of medicine but eventually also the practice of psychology, for it is from within medicine that the current practice of the Psychology Industry emerged."158 Fear appears in many of the outlier difficulties described as other symptoms.

Considering the overlap between fear and other symptoms that display themselves (see chapter 2) with the results of drugs or medications, these results should be publicized widely among those who are attempting

---

156 Ray Jungen, *A Time of Departing* (Silverton, OR: Lighthouse Trails Publishing, 2002), 52.
157 Ravi Zacharias International Ministry "Secularization, Pluralization, Privatization Part 1," Clemson University, South Carolina, viewed Sep 4, 2017. Hillsong Channel.
158 Tana Dineen, *Manufacturing Victims* (New York: Robert Davies Multimedia, 2000), 240.

to help. They may not see what is happening to their patients.

As previously mentioned, control is a crucial element for life. Control means reduced stress. Control reduces fear. When fear is reduced, it means control is present. Emergencies are never on the schedule. They are an indicator of loss of control. When soldiers lose the initiative in battle, fear is heightened. Preparation and training are a great ingredient for the ability to overcome fear with both military and civilians. Facing the enemy of the battlefield can bring fear regardless of prior preparations. Still, when the medical professionals began their tests on the brain to see reactions people have to fearful stimuli, the results are mixed. First, scientists tested the part of the brain called the amygdala. Early tests showed that the amygdala was impacted with fearful stimuli. Tests later showed that many parts of the brain were affected, and male and female results differed. After hundreds of tests, one thing was clear: "From these contrary results, it became clear to me—and ultimately to many other scientists—that the amygdala is not the home of fear in the brain."[159] Further tests also showed that "amygdala activity likewise increases during events usually considered non-emotional such as when you feel pain, learn something new, meet new people, or make decisions."[160] These are fear producers.

Based on that, doctors will diagnose generalized anxiety disorder (GAD) and prescribe benzodiazepines.

---
159 Lisa Feldman Barrett, *How Emotions Are Made* (New York: Houghton Mifflin Harcourt, 2017), 20. **Lisa Feldman Barrett, How Emotions are made (New York: Houghton Mifflin Harcourt, 2017), 20.**
160 Barrett, 22.

This is to implement healthy coping strategies by stabilizing moods. Psychiatrists most usually prescribe the medications of Lexapro and Paxil, as selective serotonin reuptake inhibitors (SSRI). Other well-known drugs are Valium, Xanax, Klonopin, Ativan. "Anxiety is physiological. But it can be lessened or worsened by the ways that you cope with it. Thus, psychotherapy for anxiety disorders is needed, especially the psychotherapies that emphasize symptom management, like cognitive-behavioral therapy, mindfulness, and the stress management therapies."[161]

Valium side effects are paranoid or suicide ideation (thoughts) and decreases in memory and judgment. Xanax side effects are drowsiness and dizziness. Other symptoms include swelling in the extremities, difficulty sleeping, memory problems, and headaches. Klonopin mirrors Xanax in its side effects with the exception of loss of appetite and slurred speech. Ativan causes the same issues, plus skin rash and nausea.[162]

Mindfulness is a fashionable meditation that is known for reducing stress, but there are drawbacks: "But scientists have discovered one potential drawback—it can lead you to remember things that haven't happened. People taking part in a 15-minute mindfulness session performed worse than those who did not sit in on a memory test, researchers found."[163]

---

161 Khoshaba, Deborah, 2012. "Are You Living with Chronic Worry and Fear?" *Psychology Today*, Aug 29. Accessed Oct 16, 2017. http://www.psychologytoday.com.
162 All information concerning prescription drug side effects come from https://www.rxlist.com.
163 TBC Staff, EN. 2015. Mindfulness Meditation Fad Popular with Celebrities Can Make You Dream Up False Memories, Accessed 16 Oct, 2017. The Berean Call. https://www.tbc.com.

As is plain to see, those who are fearful will go to great lengths to find other solutions than to go to God with their fears.

**Fear (Anxiety), Theological**

The Bible has much to say about fear, where it comes from, and how God can give fast, permanent relief to fear without side effects. The balm of Gilead cannot be applied to the skin or taken orally or injected into a vein. It must be taken into the heart by faith by one who already trusts in the Lord. The Word of God is to be the counteracting agent taken into the mind and relied upon. The Bible is to be meditated upon so that at the moment of need, the Bible can be on the mind and be used as a comfort. Solomon observes, "When thou liest down, thou shalt not be afraid: yea, thou shalt lie down, and thy sleep shall be sweet. Be not afraid of sudden fear, neither of the desolation of the wicked, when it cometh" (Prov. 3:24–25). The third chapter of Proverbs starts with and gives example after example of what the Bible can do. The benefits of knowing the law of God (v. 1), finding peace (v. 2), mercy and truth (v. 3), wisdom (v. 13). It is a matter of meditating on it day and night.

When soldiers go to war, should they begin fearing for their lives, a verse for them to be reminded of is, for example, "And fear not them which kill the body but are not able to kill the soul; but rather fear him which is able to destroy both soul and body in hell" (Matt. 10:28). When a soldier has a firm and resolute understanding of his eternal destiny, should a bullet fatally strike him, he is able to go into the combat zone unafraid. Curington says, "By humility (essence of allowing Christ to do everything through me) and the fear (respect) of the Lord are riches, and honour (esteem), and life (in perpetuity)."[164] God has promised the believer in Psalm 23:4, "Yea, though I walk through the valley of the shadow of death, I will fear no evil: for thou art with me, thy rod and thy staff they comfort me." The prayers of fellow believers are the best remedy for the fearing warrior. The actions of God taken on behalf of a soldier from a person of prayer and faith, though they are thousands of miles away, can be effective because of an omnipresent God who is able to minister at the moment of need. There has been a plethora of instances where a soldier has gone out to face the enemy in wartime, knowing that a praying mother was back home, interceding for him. This knowledge was said to have given the soldier strength to do his dangerous duty when he would have otherwise faltered. It is through prayer that the Spirit of God can provide ministry to the human spirit in those moments of fear and dread. Paul said, "For the Lord has not given us the spirit of fear, but of power, and of love, and of a sound mind" (2 Tim. 1:7).

In addressing fear, Carragher contends, "Stress causing fear is one of the greatest concerns of people facing PTSD. Often the fear is a symptom brought on by the traumas and abuse experienced previously in one's life. In other words, an individual who was shot by an enemy soldier of a certain color with certain features may fear people with those features for the rest

---

164 Steve Curington, By Humility and Fear, Dissected & Defined, Victorious Life Blog, Oct 22, 2016, accessed March 10, 2018, https://rurecovery.com.

of his life."[165] Anxiety or fear of future events can be relieved by giving control of all of life over to God. God is sovereign over every event that occurs. Where there is hope, anxiety is reduced. Peele writes concerning self-efficacy, "Efficacy is the ability to bring about desired goals."[166] It has to do with having confidence in self. In a controlled environment, self-empowerment can bring false confidence. "Self-efficacy is an important determinant of people's susceptibility to addiction."[167] Medicines that mask troubles bring about a false sense of security and control. Christ is able to give relief to the anxious fears one may have when the child of God is willing to relinquish control of those areas that trouble them and give them to God.

Fear, as stated by Thomson, is "When one is fraught with excessive fears, therefore, he is, in reality, fearing God's judgment due to sin which he is presently entertaining in his heart … it is the fear God's displeasure which is at work in his heart … for which his conscience is holding him guilty."[168] Thomson discusses anxiety as separate from fear, stating, "Fear is one's response to something specific—to a known threat—but anxiety is fear which is experienced when there appears to be no adequate reason for it."[169]

---

165  Douglas Carragher, *Wounded Spirits: A Biblical Approach to Dealing with the Effects of Post Traumatic Stress Disorder* (Murfreesboro, TN: Walden Way, 2014), 34.
166  Stanton Peele, *Diseasing of America: Addiction Treatment Out of Control* (Lexington, MA: 1989), 272.
167  Peele, 273.
168  Rich Thomson, *The Heart of Man and the Mental Disorders: How the Word of God is Sufficient,* 2d Ed. (Alief, TX: Biblical Counseling Ministries, Inc., 2012), 72.
169  Thomson, 258.

Thomson later suggests uncaused fear or anxiety has one cause: a fear of pending judgment from God for known personal wrongs that have not been made right. Illustrations can be seen in the life of Adam and Eve as they disregarded God's rule concerning the forbidden tree in Eden. Conversely, "The righteous are bold as a lion" (Prov. 28:1).

Adams contrasts fear with love. In his nouthetic style of counseling, Adams goes straight to the Scripture and expounds on 1 John 4:17, 18: "Herein is love made perfect, that we may have boldness in the day of judgment: because as he is, so are we in this world. There is no fear in love; but perfect love casts out fear: because fear hath torment. He that feareth is not made perfect in love." Adams continues, commenting, "John himself sets fear and love over against each other as mutually exclusive. While John specifically is concerned about the fear of the judgment to come and shows how love from God and for God erases all such fear his words also demand broader application."[170] This speaks to the removal of fear when there is a relationship between the redeemed sinner and Holy God.

Collins notes that there are many fears and that these are not unusual. He says that in many facets of life, many types of fear will manifest themselves. Collins empathizes with this in separate locations in his manual but gives no scriptural help. His work is recognized in books, such as *Christ Centered Therapy*.[171]

---

170 Jay E. Adams, *The Christian Counselor's Manual* (Grand Rapids: Zondervan, 1973), 413–414.
171 Neil T. Anderson, Terry E. Zuehlke, and Julianne S. Zuehlke, *Christ Centered Therapy* (Grand Rapids: Zondervan, 2000), 10.

In another case, author Neil T. Anderson also cautions those reading Christian Psychologist Larry Crabb that he does not believe a Christian has the answers for one with mental issues. Anderson comments on Crabb's approach that "The weakness of this approach, in Dr. Crabb's view, is that its advocates fail to recognize the ability of Scripture to address psychological problems such as depression, anxiety, codependency, addiction, infidelity, anger, and family conflicts."[172] As I have said before the Word of God will provide for all these problems. We don't give the Bible its due. Anderson adds, "The reality of physical death has been broken. The apostle Paul teaches that Christ's resurrection has rendered physical death important, quoting 1 Cor. 15:54–55 and Phil. 1:21."[173]

Author and college professor Jim Berg notes in his study guide dealing with fear, that uncertainty and doubt will plague the one who is not anchored in the Word of God. The mature student of the Word will be equipped to win the battle. Berg says, "These evil thoughts are immediately dismissed by a mature believer as a reminder that his heart is 'deceitful above all things, and desperately wicked,'" according to Jeremiah 17:9.[174] Our emotionally stressed issues can be overcome through faith in God and adherence to the Bible.

---

172  Anderson, 66.
173  Anderson, 269–270.
174  Berg. 40.

# CHAPTER 10

## Guilt, theoretical

Schiraldi says, "Guilt affirms morality."[175] Thus, the question, whose morality, or where does a sense of right or wrong come from? For those who attempt to live without God, they would operate under a belief of how good a procedure appears to work, called utilitarianism. Grossman says, "Fear is a specific yet brief and fleeting emotion that lies within the individual, but guilt is often long term and can belong to the society as a whole."[176] Guilt is established upon the individual when he/she has determined within their own conscience that a principle has been violated. These violations may come through particular religious or other moral teachings. Charles Figley, a PTSD authority, developed five questions that assist in coming to grips with PTSD:

"1. What happened?

2. Why did the event happen?

3. Why did I act the way I did during the event?

---

175 Schiraldi, 194.
176 Grossman, *On Killing*, 53.

4. Why have I acted the way I have since that time?
5. If something like this were to happen again, what would I do differently to cope and survive?"[177]

In attempting to answer these questions, there must be an absolute source of truth. With the current trend that no absolutes exist, all reactions and all results are up to the individual, so there is no need to adjust reactions.

These questions attempt to measure the amount of guilt someone might have in an incident. These questions are a bit subjective, and the answers will come based on one's own opinion. Experiences create opinions. Shay observes, "Much ... pertained to veterans' moral anguish over what they did or did not do in regards to their American comrades. Horrific things done to enemy soldiers and civilians have great power to injure the mind and spirit of those who have done them."[178] Many counselors do not have combat experience, thus lacking credibility in the eyes of those who have gone to war. Counselors without combat experience often struggle with asking effective questions to combat veterans. Pertinent questions concerning soldiers' stress issues assist soldiers to answer key questions and help them overcome fears. If more persons were involved, then there may be other viewpoints that change the scenario and reveal that an incident did not occur as it was first thought it did.

---

177 Schiraldi, 198.
178 Jonathan Shay, *Odysseus in America: Combat Trauma and the Trials of Homecoming* (New York: Scribner, 2002), 109–110.

There is no absolute answer that can be given because individuals are fallible and are prone to mistakes. Individuals possess biases that may weigh on their view of an incident. Some can walk away from a traumatic situation with little or no ill effect. Others may be highly traumatized. Guilt levels will vary upon individuals regardless of their level of self-blame. One who has the arbitrary rule will do the assessing, for all things are relative and non-absolute. A psychiatrist working with a veteran might begin a session with someone plagued with guilt by asking how much blame he has laid on himself. They might begin by spreading the guilt around, as it is human nature to blame others.

Codependency can be to blame. "There is generally no fault finding with self unless it is not having been good enough to self. Instead, the blame and fault finding on the person's parents for not having loved enough or just right."[179] When consoling a guilt-ridden soldier, pointing out who might be at fault, a counselor might point out that he was assigned to combat by the Department of the Army. The personnel office assigns the soldier to the combat unit, and the sergeant places the soldier on sentry duty; the soldier is then shot by the enemy while on duty. The sergeant who put him on duty cannot take the full blame. The established system in which a psychologist works is problem-centered counseling.

Noted former secular psychologist Martin Bobgan states, "The problem centered counselor needs to hear the problem explained; try to understand it according to some theory or guesswork: and offer some kind

---

179 Bobgan, *Twelve Steps to Destruction*, 1991, 152.

of solution."[180] As the psychologist occupies himself with trying to find ways to relieve guilt and remove the pain of real or imagined fault, the consequence is proving to the individual being counseled that they are entirely guiltless. The reality is that the person that was directly harmed must take some blame; somewhere they were to blame for something. Man's heart of sin portrayed in the book of Jeremiah relates easily to the way a man thinks, as stated in Proverbs 23:7, "As a man thinketh in his heart, so is he." The heart decides much about a man's attitude and action. Bobgan points out, "Read the cases in counseling books and you will see how the truth of Jeremiah 17:9 plays out. It is rare to find a person who will take responsibility for the problem without any confirmation bias" [181] [emphasis in original]. Jeremiah 17:9 says that the heart will lie. The deceived is unable to be cured except by the transformation that comes in regeneration in Christ.

The various organizations that had a part in placing that man at the place in the war at that time must take equal blame. Schiraldi uses the following steps:

"Step 1: Narrative and Self-Assessment

Step 2: Examination of Other's Direct Roles

Step 3: Examination of Others' Indirect Roles

Step 4: Reorienting Responsibilities/Blame

Step 5: Assessing Self-Punishment

Step 6: A Plan for Realistic, Proactive Amends

---

180 Martin Bobgan, *Person to Person Ministry* (Santa Barbara, Ca: EastGate Publishing, 2009), 35.
181 Bobgan, *Twelve Steps to Destruction*, 35.

Step 7: Reflection and Reframing"[182]

What we don't see in these steps is "Where is God"? The key portions of the therapy suggested involves verbalizing it, that is, talking about it. The roles of responsibility must be assessed and reassessed to include the role of the enemy in the death of the soldier. One must give an honest assessment of responsibility, direct or indirect. Another factor that may be involved is guilt versus shame. Guilt has to do with what you did. This does not take as long to solve. Shame is a questioning of who you are and what you think of yourself, which generally takes more time to change and overcome.

Schiraldi finishes the section on guilt with a portion on "Utilizing Spiritual Resources." He gives the example of the Buddhist and instructs the guilt-ridden person to "visualize" a deity that you would wish to make things right. Feelings and the object to whom you confess will take care of the rest. The repentant is to visualize the being reacting with a smile and gestures of forgiveness. The last point Schiraldi made describes the result that is advertised by New Age philosophers. Schiraldi further notes, "Visualize the light filling you until you feel yourself made up entirely of that light. You soar up into the sky and are united with the figure. Relax and enjoy the bliss of that oneness for as long as possible."[183] He invents a scenario in an attempt to ease the guilt. New Age teachers that promote a new spirituality to go alongside psychology often speak of the light that they encounter when practicing the mysticism of the New Age. It is both deceptive and demonic.

---

182 Schiraldi, 199–204.
183 Schiraldi, 210.

When make-believe events become normal, real life can become a challenge. Frustration can set in and with it, rage. Schiraldi continues in his comments about anger: "Intense anger is common in PTSD for the reason that all make sense. Normal day-to-day living rarely demands intense, extreme emotions. But during traumatic events, raw emotions are often unleashed."[184] An enemy killing a soldier's buddy can set off a level of rage in that soldier he/she never experienced before. When these extreme expressions of emotion are not reined in, they will continue and have no regard to its victim, deserving or not. Anger is seldom a self-criticizing emotion. Its target is nearly always outside oneself, while inward failures are generally overlooked. Schiraldi further adds, "Anger is a negative, uncomfortable feeling that follows some specific thoughts about something that we view as threatening or frustrating."[185] The therapist will ask the patient to put his anger into words and then to rank the sources of his anger.

When a soldier is involved in a conflict that results in numerous soldiers dying, and when he is one of few who survive, or when he survives a "close call" that killed a friend, he could develop survivor guilt. Matsakis, commenting on guilt, states that "Survivor guilt is so central to PTSD that it used to be considered one of the formal criteria for diagnosing the disorder."[186] Symptom categories change over time. Symptoms diagnosed through psychology go through constant change, depending on the psychologist; issues and

---

184  Ibid., 119.
185  Schiraldi, 120.
186  Matsakis, 330.

answers can go, says Bobgan, "through up to almost 500 varieties"[187]

Journaling is a step many therapists ask of those who struggle with anger, asking them to try to write down the feelings, thoughts, and words that started the anger process. Anger must be recognized not as a primary problem, but a reaction to something that triggered that emotion. Putting into words the injury is important. Communication with loved ones is important, getting clarification when harm occurs. Ask the person who did the supposed hurt to clarify the words, to relieve any misunderstanding. Find a kind way to express concerns. If needed, take a break from the situation and remove yourself from further provocation.

Look at the humorous side of things and begin to laugh at yourself and with others, realizing that there are times for certain kinds of anger. When someone is wronged or belittled, it could be a time for gentle arousal into constructive anger. Bobgan concludes the thought by stating, "Disturbed anger is out of control and disproportionate to the offense. Non-disturbed anger is functional (e.g., annoyance that stimulates us to rational communication, reasonable action to prevent disrespectful treatment, or problem solving.)"[188]

PTSD is often manifested in a soldier through guilt, grief, and anger when they have not dealt with it sufficiently. The three often show themselves in similar ways. In combat, fear and grief are highly discouraged emotions. They can cause the soldier to be erratic in

---

187 Bobgan, *Person to Person Ministry*, 20.
188 Bobgan, 131.

combat and slow to respond to orders, endangering the mission. Anger, however, is encouraged. It has brought out the best, for the moment, in soldiers who otherwise might not have been able to accomplish their duties in the unit. Anger is the point of expression resulting from the cumulative effect of the tour combat experience. Control or the lack thereof has a place in the stirrings of anger. Matsakis also states, "Often anger is purely anger. But anger is often also a disguise or defense against grief, confusion, fear, and the sense of powerlessness."[189] As the aspect of powerlessness is mentioned, another term that could easily replace it is "control." As mentioned before, when deployments occur, the training the soldier receives is meant in part to take and keep control of the battlefield to increase the possibilities of mission completion. Control of the battle gives those involved confidence and assists in defeating those elements of PTSD described in the preceding page.

When the authority of God is not present in a soldier's life, there is a loss of respect of God's rules, such as the Ten Commandments. Not knowing God's grace and forgiveness will result in guilt that will reside in unforgiveness within a soldier's mind and heart, stemming from combat experiences. Doubt reigns when bad decisions cost lives in battle. A soldier needs to know God's forgiveness that relieves stress and removes the need for substances that ultimately harm the mind and body. Shay reflects on his dealings with Vietnam veterans saying, "Innocents died, and

---

[189] Aphrodite Matsakis, *I Can't Get Over It* (Oakland, Ca: New Harbinger, 1992), 332.

apparently everyone involved that night feels anguished by it. Those 'gotcha' journalists who seem to believe … feeling guilty, he must be guilty are completely wrong. A person of the good moral character feels more pain—call it guilt, shame, anguish, remorse—after doing something that caused another person suffering."[190]

## Guilt, Theological

Individual guilt stems from a feeling of failure to uphold a particular standard of conduct. Man can establish rules or codes of conduct. They may coincide with God's standard, or they may be an attempt to establish a new standard. God's standard has been set, but a man's heart of rebellion requires him to establish a livable standard. When a level of conduct has been implemented for an individual or for a group that does not appease a conscience, it affects the soul (mind, will, and emotions), and one may feel that they have not achieved a level of suitable morality. God establishes specific standards for all people (see the Ten Commandments in Exodus 20 for example).

In non-essential rules for life, where God's grace is experienced, Paul writes, "Let each person be fully persuaded in his own mind" (Rom. 14:5). The counselor should be one who brings the love of God and the power of Jesus Christ into direct focus concerning the need for forgiveness and a relationship with a loving heavenly Father. Collins writes, "The Christian counselor seeks to bring people into a personal relationship with Jesus Christ and help them

---

190   Shay, *Odysseus*, 111–112.

find forgiveness and relief from the crippling effects of sin and guilt."[191] Coming to the basic component(s) of guilt, much of it is related to suffering, which can come in many different forms. Suffering can be connected to a poor marriage relationship, health issues, financial problems, addictions, loss of a loved one, and a score of other problems, whereas guilt results from how a person perceives their inability to cope with their circumstances. The theological side of guilt stems from the perceived inability to meet God's standard of morality. Collins surmises, "Divine forgiveness is a major theme, especially in the New Testament ... Although some passages of Scripture mention forgiveness without discussing repentance, other passages imply to at least two conditions must be met before God forgives."[192] As the Scriptures say, "If we confess our sins, he is faithful and just to forgive us our sins, and to cleanse us from all unrighteousness" (1 Jn. 1:9).

Guilt is masked by anger and hurt. Fear can be associated with these emotions. With so many separate emotions that can be involved, the danger of adding a mind-altering drug to the mixture usually worsens it. When the brain is not permitted to function, the soul is directly affected; and with the inability to think clearly, the problems cannot be resolved. Meditating on Scripture is a means by which the Holy Spirit can minister to those who are suffering. This also helps the sufferer to better understand God's grace as well as helping the sufferer to extend forgiveness others and

---

191 Gary R. Collins, *Christian Counseling* (Dallas: Word, 1988), 16.
192 Collins, 137.

themselves. Steve Curington writes, "God balances guilt with blame. As we accept the blame for our wrong actions, God will remove the guilt."[193]

A person can allow two things to happen to them when they are feeling guilt. They can receive the guilt from Satan and receive and act upon the condemnation that he gives, remaining defeated, or they can receive the forgiveness that comes through Jesus Christ. Doug Carragher, president of Wounded Spirits Ministries Inc. and author writes:

Condemnation comes from Satan and is meant to tear you down and ruin your life. It points out what a failure you are and how badly you have messed up your life. It is constantly showing you the problem but never presents the solution ... The Bible teaches that with our Lord the opposite is true. Remember, the Lord did not to condemn the world; he came to save it. (John 12:47)[194]

Just as it is beneficial to the warrior to win the battle in a firefight under control, it is also beneficial to ease stressful situations when a mother can talk calmly to her children and direct them when she has control of her emotions. Self-control is Spirit-control. "A soft answer turneth away wrath: but grievous words stir up anger" (Prov. 15:1). Christian author and counselor Jay E. Adams contends, "There are always at least two points at which a person can stop an action: 1. At the

---

193 Steven Curington, *Reformers Unanimous: Stronghold Handbook* (Rockford: IL: Steven Boyd Publishing), nd.
194 Carragher, 45.

point of resistance. 2. At the point of restraint."[195] Anger can be used as a defensive mechanism. As Anderson explains, "They hang on to their anger as a means of protecting themselves from being hurt again, but in reality, they are only hurting themselves. To forgive is to set a captive free, and only when we forgive do we discover that we are the captive."[196] If forgiveness is genuine, there is freedom; if it is not genuine, he is turned over to the tormentor (Matt. 18:34). The removal of guilt can only come from God, for God is the originator of all morality and ethics. Be right with God, and you will be right.

Anger is an emotion that has validation. Thomson says it is "an emotion generated in man's brain and body by the attitude of his heart. And for this attitude, he is responsible to God. This is not, however, the viewpoint of human wisdom. Human wisdom asserts that since anger is simply a physical emotion, one is not responsible for having angry feelings."[197] Thomson continues, stating what makes anger right or wrong is not having anger but rather what is done with it and how it is expressed. "Be angry and yet do not sin" is expressed more than once in the Scriptures. Anger is not wrong; it is the way in which it is expressed that is. Thomson goes further and states, "Godly anger is anger for God's honor. Let one remember that godly anger is not godly because one's anger is controlled

---

195 Jay E. Adams, *The Christian Counselor's Manual* (Grand Rapids: Zondervan, 1973), 197.
196 Neil T. Anderson, and Terry E. Zuehlke, and Julianne S. Zuehlke, *Christ Centered Therapy* (Grand Rapids: Zondervan, 2000), 155.
197 Thomson, 405.

and is expressed in a positive way. Godly anger is godly because it is *concerned with God's honor, not one's own honor.*"[198] [emphasis in original.]

---

198  Ibid., 415.

# Chapter 11

## Nightmares and Flashbacks, theoretical

Aphrodite Matsakis claims in the introduction to her tome on PTSD that "you will probably need the assistance of caring friends, other survivors, and qualified professionals in understanding and meeting the challenges the trauma has thrust upon you."[199] Matsakis also believes this about where power lies. She states, "The pace at which you heal will be your own, determined by the natural healing powers within you. The purpose of this book is merely to stimulate and support the healing power that is already within you."[200] There is a hint of humanistic self-help.

Dreams, nightmares, and flashbacks are a common occurrence to those with PTSD. Interrupted sleep due to nightmares can persist for a long time. Fear, anxiety, grief, and other emotions may be part of the disruption that is experienced. To counteract these disrupted sleep patterns, some sufferers may try alcohol, thinking it will put one into a deep-enough sleep that the nightmares will not be able to come to mind. Flashbacks are of the

---
199 Matsakis, xxiii.
200 Ibid., xxiii.

same variety of the nightmare, but they occur during waking hours. One with flashbacks might suddenly drift off in their mind to an event that caused trauma. A flashback can be so overwhelming that all that a person can do is relive the events, complete with all the emotions that traumatized them initially. Flashbacks or nightmares are not just something experienced by a combat veteran. Anyone that has been through something traumatic can experience these intrusive thoughts. Matsakis gives insight states, "Flashbacks tend to occur among persons who have had to endure situations where there was an intense, chronic, or pervasive loss of security and lack of safety."[201] A continuous theme seems to be repeated concerning trauma; a loss of personal control in some fashion occurs with it.

Reactions to trauma can occur in random order, or they can come in predictable cycles. It could take weeks after an event, or it could be months or even years later, that the memories return to haunt the sufferer. Often a trigger event, something smelled, heard, said, or seen can trigger a traumatic memory. These can bring a feeling of numbness or cause one to fly into a rage. It is often called psychic or emotional numbing. Some find isolation to be the way to avoid the trigger that brings on an episode, sparing embarrassments. Toffolo, Smeets, and van den Hout collaborated in trigger effects saying:

> …odours to spontaneously trigger autobiographical memories which are highly vivid detailed, and affectively toned

---
201  Ibid., 14.

has been widely known as the Proust Phenomenon ... which may have special significance for people with Post-Traumatic Stress Disorder, who typically experience very detailed and emotional recollection of traumatic events. Clinicians have indeed noted that specific traumatic related smells (e.g., blood, diesel, Old Spice aftershave) can be powerful precipitants of traumatic memories of patients with PTSD.[202]

The senses are aroused in traumatic moments and jars the memory to relive the pain. Avoidance or isolation causes other problems, particularly if there is family around or business that needs tending. Mary Beth Williams and Soili Paijula recommend that someone with numbness or avoidance issues begin a process to eliminate them. They state:

> As you process your traumatic events ... you will see that numbing will become less necessary. If you numb because you are afraid of feeling the emotions associated with what happened to you, then it is important that you begin to allow yourself to feel in little doses. If you are extremely anxious, you may want to take medication to help reduce that anxiety.[203]

---

202 Marieke B.J. Toffolo, Monique A.M. Smeets and Marcel A. van den Hout. "Proust Revisited: Odours as Triggers of Aversive Memories," *Psychology Press* 26 no.4 (2012): 83, accessed March 15, 2018, http://ed.a.ebscohost.comeds.pdfviewer?vid.
203 Mary Beth Williams, and Soili Poijula, *The PTSD Workbook* (Oakland, CA: New Harbinger, 2002), 73.

Schiraldi adds:

> Avoidance is a hallmark of anxiety. We try to flee things that trigger it. This avoidance brings temporary relief but at quite a cost. First, we maintain the fear of the triggers … the antidote to avoidance is to face the things we fear and flow with the symptoms until the stress response runs its course and we retrain our nervous system to be less reactive. [204]

Sleep cycles generally run every four hours, allowing Rapid Eye Movement (REM) to take place. In most combat duty or shift work in the military, four hours on and four hours off is the routine. Age will determine to what extent a person's body will move when they experience REM. For those with intense combat experiences during sleep, body movements can even become dangerous for those who are sharing the bed with them. Commenting on REM, Dewey states, "They have intense battle dreams during REM sleep and cry out or move. Their wives report that it can be dangerous to sleep with them when they are having battle dreams."[205] Lessened sleep at night means poor concentration and irritability during the day. Eight hours is generally the prescribed amount of sleep, but combat vets do not have that luxury. Medications can be of some benefit to help a soldier sleep at those times when sleep escapes them. Dewey has noted, "Most of the vets I see have difficulty sleeping at least occasionally

---

204 Schiraldi, 14.
205 Larry Dewey, *War and Redemption* (Burlington, VT: Ashgate Publishing Ltd, 2004), 166.

and request for insomnia. I prescribed variety of medications for them. What helps any particular vet depends on the side effects he experiences, his response and his other symptoms."[206] There are no set reactions to medications. Everyone reacts differently. Unfortunately, prescribed medications will cause problems that last beyond the immediate benefits of duties performed.

Dangers lie in dependency on sleep aids, followed by something to keep them awake when they are on duty. For the short-term, they control symptom-relieving issues. A Vietnam vet named Bill told his group in therapy one day a story as retold by psychologist Ed Tick. Tick recounts: "The VA hospital has given me dozens of different pills in every combination for sleep, nightmares, nerves, stress, depression, and every PTSD symptom you could name … tell me why none of it ever worked."[207] This kind of testimony can be repeated over and over again. Veterans have often found that a return to the scene of the event that brought on PTSD can relieve some symptoms. Renewing and reshaping of people and places that brought on the stress can be of some use. As a result, trips to Normandy Beach, France, and Vietnam have become popular in an attempt to recapture the location of the events and defeat them, casting out ghosts of memories.

**Nightmares and Flashbacks, Theological**

The Bible's way to relieve stress that has entered the soul is coming back into the trauma through Christ

---
206  Dewey, 167.
207  Tick, *War of the Soul*, 191.

and the work that He accomplished as He died on the cross. His crucifixion was His significant action, facing trauma for His own, that resolved all the issues of PTSD. Jesus explained that there must be death that there might be a new normal in the resurrection. Jesus himself made an important statement concerning one giving up their life: "Verily, verily, I say unto you, except a corn of wheat fall into the ground and die, it abideth alone, but if it die it bringeth forth much fruit" (John 12:24). Klink states, "For a seed to be effective—to do what a seed is intended to do—it must die, otherwise it remains alone, that is it will remain a seed."[208]

As Klink comments further, Jesus took the concept a step further. "Jesus's explanation now connects the seed with the fruit, that is, the death of the Son with the life of the children of God."[209] The Scripture says, "He that loveth his life shall lose it; and he that hateth his life in this world shall keep it unto life eternal" (John 12:25). This is a new way of thinking. God wants to give us a new normal. The new life in Jesus Christ is available because of His trauma for us on the cross. He was resurrected, and He promises all that believe on Him will be resurrected one day also. This is God's plan for a new normal. Adsit attempts to soothe the troubled, giving hope, saying, "What God now has in mind is a 'new normal' for you … you are on your way to level of existence that will be better than ever."[210]

---

208 Edward W. Klink III, *John*, vol. 4 of the *Exegetical Commentary on the New Testament*, ed. Clinton E. Arnold (Grand Rapids: Zondervan, 2016), 551.
209 Klink, 552.
210 Adsit, 131.

Romans 12:2 states that the answer is a renewing of the mind, that is, a new way of thinking. Dunn states, "but as a reminder that for Paul spiritual renewal of the people must begin in the inwardness of a person ... and must include not least the person's power of thought and reason."[211] Second Corinthians 5:17 speaks of being a new creature if you are in Christ. Old things pass away; all things become new. Hughes comments, "The expression 'in Christ' sums up as briefly and as profoundly as possible the inexhaustible significance of man's redemption. It speaks of security in Him who has Himself borne in His own body the judgment of God against our sin."[212] Maybe you thought you should have died on the battlefield. Maybe you have moments when you wish you were dead, rather than going through this awful pain in PTSD and other injuries. When Christ died for sin and reconciled believers to Himself, He redeemed the soul and the spirit and will one day change the vile, sinful human body that it may be glorified. All of it will be changed.

While Paul the apostle was in a jail in Philippi, he wrote, "For I have learned, whatsoever state I am, therewith to be content" (Phil 4:11). Learning to be content while jailed is learning how to allow the Spirit to control your attitude toward your environment. Bible commentator Gaebelein explains, "It is significant that Paul had to 'learn' this virtue. Contentment is not

---

211 James D. G. Dunn, *Romans 9–16* vol. 38B of the *Word Biblical Commentary*, ed. Bruce M. Metzger (Dallas: Word, 1988), 718.
212 Philip E. Hughes. *The New International Commentary on The New Testament. The Second Epistle of the Corinthians* (Grand Rapids: Eerdmans, 1962), 202.

natural to most of mankind."[213] "Renewing of the mind (not the brain), that ye may prove what is that good, and acceptable, and perfect will of God" (Rom. 12:2b). Paul had close friendships with many who helped when he was in need and experiencing traumatizing times. Jesus, when he was experiencing traumatizing times on the cross, lost his closest friend—his Father. "My God, My God, why hast thou forsaken me?" (Matt. 27:46b). Jesus felt as though the Father had turned his back on His Son.

God wishes to walk with you through your traumatic event. Put the memory of the traumatic events down on paper, journaling, taking daily notes. Pray before you begin and pray throughout. Have a Bible nearby with some soothing Psalms to read if the memories should get too intense. God does not want you to go it alone. Adsit pleads with the PTSD sufferer: "Jesus Christ wants access to every area of your life—not to impose himself and dominate you, but to bring healing and victory. Like a patrol in Fallujah searching from house to house, checking every nook, cranny and shadow for terrorists, he wants to enter even your darkest, most ominous corners in order to conquer the foes lurking there."[214] The hidden corners are where the nightmares live. Giving everything to Jesus will bring about true healing and remove all hurtful memories.

This is a matter for Scripture meditation, allowing God to permeate the mind with his thoughts.

---

213 Frank E. Gaebelein, in "*Ephesians—Philemon,*" vol 11, of *The Expositors Bible Commentary* (Grand Rapids: Zondervan, 1979), 154.
214 Adsit, 62.

Meditation is the key to the renewing of the mind. Placing God's Word into the middle of your mental (soulish) conflict will bring victory. Again, I know more than one case when the waking mind and soul listen to Scripture all night while the body sleeps. The result is a refreshed mind that has the experience of fitting sleep for the body. For whatever troubles someone has, God can bring a soothing for those ready to receive it. Nightmares come from an overabundance of fretting and worry. As a troubled mind tries to rest, thoughts plague it, and fears cause dismay. The reassurance of the loving power of God and His omnipotence that overcomes all enemies is a must to bring healing.

Proverbs 3:24–25 gives the peace that is needed. Solomon reminds us, "When thou liest down, thou shalt not be afraid: yea, thou shalt lie down, and thy sleep shall be sweet. Be not afraid of sudden fear, neither of the desolation of the wicked, when it cometh." To be unafraid in all circumstances is a promise of an opportunity. Perfect peace is not a guarantee, but to those who choose to be reminded of God's provision when the moments of anxiety come God's presence is guaranteed and with it, peace. It is not automatic, without an effort on the part of the individual. Garrett explains, "The righteous can be free of the anxiety that plagues the wicked (vv. 23–25). Verse 23 is a general promise; it is not a guarantee that the wise will never have occasion to stumble."[215]

---

215 Duane A. Garrett, *The New American Commentary: Proverbs, Ecclesiastes, Song of Solomon* (Nashville: Broadman, 2002), 83.

Some in psychology wish for the counselee to go back in time, sometimes through the use of hypnotism, to recall past events in order to unlock past experiences so that blame and guilt can be found. Bobgan explains, "Because of the nature of memory, remembering the past cannot be done without enhancing, embellishing, omitting, or creating details to fill in the blanks. Therefore, this is a faulty method of help because of the brain's limited ability to remember accurately and its tendency to distort."[216] Paul reminds the believer that the Christian's mind is about "forgetting those things which are behind, and reaching forth unto those things which are before, I press toward the mark for the prize of the high calling of God in Christ Jesus" (Phil 3:13b–14). As F.C. Cooke explains, "(Those are not forgotten, but remembered to be renounced); but rather, the completed portion of his Christian course."[217] Paul gives a curious yet apt description of the thing that he is to do. "reaching forth [is] a graphic word descriptive of the attitude of the runner—the body thrown forward the hand outstretched, in eager straining for the prize."[218] Bobgan adds, "Witchdoctors, Sufi practitioners, shamans, Hindus, Buddhists, and yogis have practiced hypnosis, and now medical doctors, dentists, psychotherapists, and others have joined them."[219] Those who have used counterfeit means to confuse those of the Christian faith, who have not

---

216 Bobgan, *Person to Person Ministry*, 61.
217 J. Gwynn, "Philippians," in *Romans to Philemon, vol. IX* of *The Bible Commentary*, es. F.C. Cook. (Grand Rapids: Baker Book, 1981), 626.
218 Gwynn, 626.
219 Bobgan, *Person to Person Ministry*, 5.

studied the Word of God, are able to make many fall into false and even demonic practices. Those without the Lord to guide them will also fall without the use of proper discernment.

# Chapter 12

## Anger, theoretical

There was a time in life when it seemed people were generally happy. Somewhere, somehow, someone removed the fun from life. Life is now stressful. The pressures of life now seem to be everywhere. There never seems to be time for rest. Things feel rushed, hurried, and under pressure. Anger arises with the constant demands that life presents. If someone did not like their occupation, they would at, the end of the day, be able to come home to peace. Not anymore. Workplace violence increases, and domestic violence is on the rise.

America has become a violent place. The Bureau of Labor Statistics publishes: "Homicides accounted for 10 percent of all fatal occupational injuries in the United States in 2016. There were 500 workplace homicides in 2016, an increase of 83 cases from 2015."[220] In discussing the issues related to the United States and the increase in anger expressed within

---

220 Bureau of Labor Statistics. 2018, "There were 500 workplace homicides in the United States in 2016," Accessed June 18, 2018. http://www.bls.gov.

its citizenry, Crabb adds, "Instead of being a kind, compassionate nation, we are now a nation that is full of anger, frustration, impatience, and disrespect."[221] The American people have set their schedule, things to get done; the list is long, tightly compacted, with little room for error. Any deviation from the hurried and harried plan for the day is met with anger and even rage. The examples we follow are all around us in violent movies and television, usually due to one party pitting themselves against another party for supremacy. In the military, it is expressed exponentially: long hours, a tough training regimen with the fear of possible death in an impending war standing in the way.

Matsakis recommends dealing with anger in doses. Do not deal with all of it all at once, she states. "You need to try to examine one piece at a time, in small, manageable doses."[222] Matsakis breaks down into two manageable pieces how to focus on overcoming anger. One is to see the anger you may have toward yourself. Another is to focus on the anger that may be aimed at others. Matsakis relates anger at self or self-blame to guilt or survivor guilt, saying, "Some of [former prisoners of wars'] self-blame stems from feelings of powerlessness, trapped in the POW camps, and there was nothing they could do to improve their situation. They experienced intense hatred—not only toward their captors for the death of their comrades but toward themselves for being unable to help."[223] Loss of control in a highly intense circumstance produced anger and

---

221 Crabb, *Anger* (Rockford, IL: Reformers Unanimous, 2010), 10.
222 Matsakis, 175.
223 Ibid., 176.

rage, as though there was a subconscious notion that they were a victim in violation of a moral code.

Others in early psychology, such as Alfred Adler, a protégé of Freud, differed in their approach. Ehrenberg claimed, "From [the capacity of the body to compensate for organic damage], he developed his basic thesis that all human striving is directed toward compensating for feelings of inferiority … the striving for superiority and power."[224] The desire to control your environment was key to all other aspects of health: mental and physical. Again, control is the key.

An interesting definition given by Schiraldi is: "Anger is a negative, uncomfortable feeling that follows from specific thoughts about something that we view as threatening or frustrating."[225] The above definition is interesting because it stems from a premise of loss of control and sometimes involves avoidance of pain; perhaps it could be related to fear. Schedules may get interrupted by a miscalculation by self or others. Dineen says, "Grieving leads directly to anger that must be developed and targeted at the perceived perpetrator, the family, or anyone else deemed to be complicit in the 'crime.'"[226] She later comments that psychology encourages personal empowerment mostly through rendering others powerless through accusation. While Schiraldi begins with the patient by having them list justifiable versus unjustifiable anger, he asks the patient to rank the irritations and determine the good and

---

224 Otto Ehrenberg and Miriam Ehrenberg. *The Psychotherapy Maze: A Consumer's Guide to Getting In and Out of Therapy* (New York: Simon and Schuster, 1986), 33.
225 Schiraldi, 120.
226 Dineen, 224.

the bad, writing down the irritants. Schiraldi says to take responsibility, identify the anger, and after gaining composure, put it into words. These and other tips are all based upon the self-help philosophy. The patient is directed by the clinician to look deep within him/herself to find the irritants and begin taking control.

### Anger, Theological

Jesus had a solution and also explained where the problem stemmed.

> There is nothing from without a man, that entering into him can defile him: but the things which come out of him, those are they that defile the man. For from within, out of the heart of man, proceed evil thoughts, adulteries, fornications, murders, thefts, covetousness, wickedness, deceit, lasciviousness, and an evil eye, blasphemy, pride, foolishness. (Mark 7:15, 21–22)

Crabb writes about anger saying, "Anger is truly a heart disease (the heart being the seat of the emotions and a part of our soul)."[227] By understanding the roots of anger and knowing how God can help resolve this problem, it will be solved. Anger management will not solve the problem as it teaches the person to bottle up anger. It is not to put anger in a cage, as it were, but rather to get to the root of it. The differences in understanding the problem with anger are not in the brain; they are in the soul. Understanding anger is about the mind and its programming. When disturbances arise, it is the choice that comes from a God-controlled mind

---

227 Crabb, *Anger*, 13.

that makes the difference. The brain reacts according to the programming from the mind. The brain and the soul are not the same. Crabb explains, "The choices made in our souls (mind, will, and emotions) are what determines the neurochemical signal that is sent from the brain (body) to the peripheral nervous system to the muscular skeletal system of the body."[228] Defeating anger can take a lifetime. God will work His grace in the individual until the day of death. Each situation God allows will bring one closer to God, assuring love and forgiveness.

Adams quickly points out that anger is not necessarily a bad thing. Paul reminds Christians in Ephesians 4:26a, "Be angry and sin not." The Psalmist points out that, "God is angry with the wicked every day," (Psa. 7:11). Jesus also had moments when he was righteously angry. Adams reminds the reader, "Righteous anger can become unrighteous anger in two ways: (1) by the ventilation of anger; (2) by the internalization of anger."[229] Venting is to allow emotions to flow. Proverbs 29:11 directs an angry person to vent emotions in anger appropriately. Solomon reminds the reader, "A fool uttereth all his mind: but a wise man keepeth it in till afterwards." Internalizing anger can be damaging to the body and soul through added stress to the body and in the mind by creating bitterness and other hurtful attitudes.

Anger is generally viewed as an emotion that is to be avoided. Anger does not blend well with God's righteousness, and few people are able to control this

---

228  Crabb, 25.
229  Adams, *Christian Counselor Manual*, 349.

emotion profitably. Tenney expounds on anger: "Anger is forbidden to the Christian as one of the works of the flesh (Gal. 5:19–21) or as the clothing of the old nature to be put off (Col. 3:8). Christians should be slow to anger, which does not accord with God's righteousness (Jas. 1:19–20) and which hinders true prayer, (1 Tim. 2:8)."[230]

Concerning anger, Jim Berg observes that frustration, fear, and hurt are often contributors. Due to unbelief, a victim of anger will not see God as a key ingredient in life. Instead, they will focus on their own desires. When dealing with anger, Berg advises, "1. Confess the unbelief and selfish discontent exposed by the anger. 2. Do not allow the anger to continue since it is destructive. 3. Put out the fires that fuel the anger—frustration, hurt and fear."[231] Wayne Mack clarifies issues concerning anger by stating that not all anger is bad. "There are many times in Scripture when God—who cannot sin—is said to be angry. Psalm 7:11 says, "God … has indignation every day"[232] (ESV).

Mentioned above was the case of having control. Anger resides in loss of control. When we make our plans and they are unexpectedly thwarted, many times in cases of emergencies, anger can arise. Having the mind of Christ is crucial here. Examine the gospels when Jesus encountered Satan, and his reaction was one of total submitting to the Father's will. Satan tried to disrupt Jesus; he will do it to you. Submit all plans

---

230 Merrill C. Tenney, *The Zondervan Encyclopedia of the Bible*, vol 1 (Grand Rapids: Zondervan, 2009), 192.
231 Berg, 51.
232 Wayne A. Mack, *Anger and Stress*, (Phillipsburg, PA: Calvary Press, 2004), 189 Kindle.

to God. He is sovereign. He is in total control. God does not say "Oops." He makes no mistakes. Thank God each time you had plans all laid out and they went well. Everything fell into place. Thank him when they don't. God has a plan.

# CHAPTER 13

## Isolation or Avoidance, theoretical

Matsakis says, "Due to the phenomenal recording ability of the human mind, when something arises in the present that reminds you of a past event, you may feel the feelings associated with the past event."[233] These traumatic events, when they produce harmful memories, are called triggers. When a traumatic event occurs, the mind will pick out certain elements involved in the traumatizing event and hard wire them into the subconscious, and these memories will become triggers. Whenever these memories, whether they be sights, sounds, smells, tastes, or even an anniversary date of an event, reoccur in the mind, they will return to the memory to haunt the individual. A PTSD sufferer will then do all that they can to isolate from the triggers that bring back memories. Sang says, "Isolation is an abnormal psychopathology to humans. Isolation is not a pathological symptom but isolation is a phenomenon of pathological factor or situation, and it may be the only survival method to someone ... But isolation of post-traumatic stress disorder is ego-

---

233 Matsakis, 103.

dystonic, so this patient suffers from social isolation."[234] With isolation or avoidance comes attempts at relief from the haunting memories. For many with avoidance issues, the memories will still haunt them and are generally accompanied by the supposed need for alcohol or other narcotics in an attempt to deaden the pain.

Feeling safe is an important priority to one with PTSD. At times dissociation can occur. Dissociation occurs when a potentially traumatizing memory comes to the person. The traumatized person will change the thought by changing their location, activity, or anything that will take their mind away from the traumatic memory. Schiraldi says, "Dissociation is a defense against extremely distressful, painful experience. The mind walls off trauma material to try to contain it in much the same way as the body walls off infection. Dissociation is most likely to occur if the trauma was severe, repeated, or occurred at a very young age."[235] Dissociation can come in the form of depersonalization (separate oneself from the trauma as an outside observer); amnesia (forgetting parts of trauma); flashbacks (falling back into memories without control of them); fugue (travel to a destination not knowing how he got there); or dissociative identity disorder (DID) (someone with two personalities).

Avoidance can also be called numbing. Sometimes the evidence of pain can come forth as simply a desire

---

234 Sang-Bin Baek, "Psychopathology of Social Isolation," *Journal of Exercise Rehabilitation,* June 19, 2014, accessed June 22, 2018, http://www.ncbi.nim.nih.gov.

235 Schiraldi, 22.

to not speak about an event. Many soldiers return from war and will not speak about their activities. A numbing or avoidance can result in an amnesia-like symptom. As explained by Schiraldi, "One person might obsess over worries or physical pain in order to avoid facing painful feelings. Another might use anger to avoid facing deeper feelings."[236] There may also be trouble with a veteran of war with attempting to express love, or they may have trouble with other emotions, such as learning to laugh or cry at appropriate times.

Having control of one's emotions is a socially acceptable thing. The inability to keep from crying at times when a trigger occurs can be embarrassing. Knowing when to laugh or cry may seem simple, but when control is lost, it can cause one to isolate out of fear of embarrassment. Schiraldi points out, "People with PTSD commonly feel detached or estranged from others. People who have endured combat, rape, disaster work, and other forms of trauma often assume that they are now different and that no one could possibly relate to their experiences."[237] One may never laugh or cry while others might do either without reason or controls. Schiraldi reveals, "As trauma can lead one to feel disconnected from others, it can also lead one to feel ones to be disconnected to his or her future. This is called a sense of foreshortened future ... victims can't envision or look forward to a normal, happy future ... it is difficult making plans for the future. Instead, their pessimistic expectations for the future might include disasters, repetition of the trauma, dying young or

---

236  Schiraldi, 10.
237  Ibid., 10.

simply finding no joy."[238] Memories can intrude and disrupt plans for projects, big or small. This writer knows of these episodes personally.

**Isolation or Avoidance, Theological**

These symptoms of isolation and avoidance are derived for a lack of recognizing God's complete love for them and control. The Christian often loses sight of who the enemy is and how that enemy is to be defeated. Paul gives insight saying:

> Finally, my brethren, be strong in the Lord, and in the power of his might. Put on the whole armor of God, that ye may be able to stand against the wiles of the devil. For we wrestle not against flesh and blood, but against principalities, against powers, against the rulers of the darkness of this world, against spiritual wickedness in high places. (Eph. 6:10–12)

F.C. Cook brings out: "Rather, 'be strengthened,' the pieces of armour, enumerated below will be useless unless a Divine strength is imparted to wear and use them."[239] The Bible goes on to answer how to defeat this enemy: the whole armor of God is the solution. When the focus is on the problem and fear invades because it is believed the fight is emotional, the focus is lost as to the real enemy. When fears overwhelm, there is no place to go but to the Lord. David, the warrior, said:

> When my spirit was overwhelmed within me, then thou newest my path. In the

---
238 Ibid., 11.
239 F.C. Cook, 575.

way wherein I walked have they privily laid a snare for me. I looked on my right hand, and behold, but there was no man that would know me: refuge failed me no man cared for my soul. I cried unto thee, O Lord: I said, thou are my refuge and my portion in the land of the living. (Psa. 142:3–5)

These verses describe the inner depths of a soldier's soul in and after war. David experienced it and was able, through the Holy Spirit, to write it in this psalm for the readers' instruction. These are precious verses. Jones states, "Distress is part of man's nature where it is most severely felt ... If the spirit be peaceful and blessed, if it inspired by joy and hope, it enables man to triumph over the severest physical suffering."[240] A soldier can read these verses and gain a comradery with one who has suffered. When a soldier feels that they need to hide from things that make them afraid, they need to go to the Lord and hide in Him as David did.

When Saul chased David, David wrote a psalm to reflect his anxious thoughts. The psalmist writes, "Deliver me, O Lord from my enemies: I flee unto thee to hide me" (Psa. 143:9). When there is a felt need to hide or isolate, do it in God: "God is our refuge and strength, a very present help in trouble" (Psa. 46:1). The psalmist equates this trouble with the nations in warfare and with the uproar of the environment. The wars and the natural catastrophes are what, in part,

---

240 William Jones, J.W. Burns and George Barlow. *The Preacher Complete Homiletic Commentary.* (Grand Rapids: Baker, 1978), 400.

causes PTSD. For one to know God's power and yet to know God's love is the beginning of knowing that there is hope in Him and that He can answer all questions and solve all problems. "He maketh wars to cease" (Psa. 46:9a). As Jamieson explains, "When he has destroyed the ambitious world-powers which caused wars, then peace ensues."[241] Trust must be in the Lord to give the victory, not only on the physical battlefield but also on the battlefield of the soul.

---

241 Jamieson, Faucette, Brown, *A Commentary, Critical, Experimental and Practical Vol II* (Grand Rapids: Eerdman, 1978), 202.

# CHAPTER 14

## Pain and Suffering, theoretical

It is the physician's routine to attempt to reduce the levels of pain that their patients suffer and to remove the amount of discomfort that accompanies many illnesses and injuries. When one enters the physician's office, they are given a series of tests that determine the patient's current condition. An added element to the screening is a simple question: "What is your current level of pain?" While the patient is asked, he or she is generally looking in the direction of a wall-mounted chart that provides pictures of faces displaying different levels of discomfort, with numbers ranging from one to ten. A physician has been trained to give a high regard to the patient's pain level. The opioid epidemic is the result of much of this issue of pain. The desire to escape pain has resulted in a plethora of pain killers in the pharmaceutical market. Kathryn Martin says, "Although there are basic physiological processes involved in pain, individuals differ in the ways that the pain sensory information is interpreted and experienced."[242]

The topic of pain management has been given over to the health care professional to address since the religious and philosophical world seemed to come up empty in giving a viable response. Widely known, late apologist Ravi Zacharias says:

One does not have to be a profound philosopher to feel this deeply as the most soul-felt of all questions to God. But as we think of the question, one must question the question. G.K. Chesterton summed up this counterpoint well when he suggested that when belief in God becomes difficult, the tendency is to turn away from him—but in heaven's name to what?"[243]

In attempting to determine the body's processing of pain, researchers have theorized, "a system of transmissions of nerve impulses from afferent fibers to spinal cord transmission that is modulated by a gating mechanism in the spinal dorsal horn known as Gate Control Theory of Pain."[244] The mechanism highlights the role of the mind and psychological factors. As man's ability to advance in the science and knowledge of the psychological theories, verifiable information will come and go, and new methods will be explored. Suicides are still a concern, and new and more effective therapies for suicide prevention are currently being studied. There is a segment of the military population that suffers from PTSD. They have a measure of relief for a time with the

---

242 Kathryn Leigh Martin, "The Influence of Pain Avoidance on the Experience of Mindfulness Training" (Dr. Psy, Alliant University, 2012), 2.
243 Zacharias, *Beyond Opinion,* 181.
244 Martin, 5.

techniques that they have employed. Suicides, as well as homelessness, continue to rise, however, for those who have departed the service.

Veterans Administration Hospitals have their challenges in attempting to assist the veteran. Dave Boyer comments sadly, "Two years after the scandal emerged over the phony waiting lists for patients at the Department of Veterans Affairs facility in Phoenix, the department is still beset with problems ranging from fresh accusations of falsified waiting lists to system-wide failure to discipline wrongdoing."[245]

**Pain and Suffering, Theological**

World religions have, in their various ways, attempted to answer the questions of suffering. Zacharias notes, "Buddhism was founded because of the nature of suffering."[246] In Christianity, God got personally involved, not avoiding the issue but rather sharing in it. Clinton White explains, "The greatest example of suffering is found in the story of the crucifixion of Jesus Christ. Christ's death on the cross with its intense physical agony while bearing God's wrath for the sins of the world was the greatest calamity to have come upon a human being."[247] The suffering of Jesus Christ went beyond the pain of the physical; it was a sorrow that was added to due to suffering for the sin of mankind that would be meted out in

---

245 Dave Boyer, "VA still plagued by problems two years after scandal," *Washington Times,* April 3, 2016.
246 Zacharias, *Beyond Opinion,* 182.
247 Clinton Alexander White, "Training Army Chaplains to Provide Biblical Counseling to Soldiers with Post Traumatic Stress Disorder" (DMin diss, Southern Baptist Theological Seminary, 2013), 9.

terms of eternal torture. The suffering servant picture of the Lord Jesus Christ portrayed in Isaiah 53 is key to understanding God's purpose and plan in suffering. Many today are not able to comprehend enduring any level of suffering in any form, deserved or not.

Luke says, "And he said to them all, if any man will come after me, let him deny himself, and take up his cross daily, and follow me" (Luke 9:23). Sorrow and suffering are part and parcel of the Christian life. James Brooks adds, "Self-denial is taking up the cross, the one who takes up the cross is denying self … those who do not mortify self-sovereignty cannot be his disciples."[248] Many are attempting to escape pain and suffering by any means possible. Medications and Eastern religion techniques, as mentioned earlier, are thought to be the solution. Medication, in particular, has proven to be the death of many. The Bible, as it so often does, brings forth the truth to this issue. Brooks continues, "Self-denial is cross-bearing and this second imperative, take up his cross intimates that being Jesus' disciple will not be a painless venture … The one who took up the cross was on a one-way journey to horrendous pain and death."[249] Daily self-denial in some form that differs with each believer is God's intended reality. This thinking will repulse the unbeliever because he is in spiritual darkness. The Bible states that one intention behind the medication is to be the final step in preparing one for death. Back at the time of Proverbs, alcohol or strong drink could be a medication. Solomon explains, "Give strong drink unto him that is ready to perish, and

---

248 James William Brooks, Jr, "The Divine Design of Christian Suffering: Mortification, Maturation, and Glorification," (Southern Baptist Seminary, 2016), 91.
249 Brooks, 95.

wine unto those that are of a heavy heart" (Prov. 31:6). Alcohol and like medications were given as hospice-styled assistance upon death, making the final hours painless and was not intended as a level-one treatment.

God directed his followers that through the example of Jesus Christ, a measure of suffering was to be part of life. No life was intended to be pain-free simply because of the fact of the curse of sin through man's fall. Walking close to God will not remove the pain but will supply hope and perhaps some reasoning behind the infliction of such pain. Yet "Man is born unto trouble as the sparks fly upward" (Job 5:7). Pain is an amazing gift. Pain is given to each person as a warning devise to let one know that danger is present. Discomfort gives us the ability to learn about harmful things in our vicinity to gain insight into ways to avoid further damage. When stressors hit the mental and physical system, discomfort comes as a warning that something needs fixing.

In the pain-relief culture that so many live in, it is no wonder that so many are fully engaged in finding relief of any ache or pain, which slows their daily progress toward purpose. Physicians and psychiatrists have an ever-watchful eye toward those things that can relieve pain at a moment's notice. Pain has its purpose. One hundred people in the world suffer from cognitive insensitivity to pain with anhidrosis (CIPA). Zacharias concludes, "The victim does not feel any pain, nor … sweat or shed tears … life … is one of perpetual danger. The average lifespan for a CIPA child is twenty-five years. Parents of children with CIPA have one prayer: that they would feel pain."[250]

---

250 Zacharias, *Beyond Opinion*, 188–189.

# Conclusion

When considering the many issues that arise as PTSD symptoms are discussed, an important final word must be provided: *sanctification*. Sanctification is the answer to the various issues people face when contending with PTSD. Allowing God into all aspects of one's life will bring strained emotions under the control of the Holy Spirit. Each time an issue arises and it is given over in thought and deed to the dominion of the Holy Spirit, victory will be the result. Powlison speaks of the importance of sanctification when he describes the topic in nine ways, saying:

> Remember that God is sovereign … remind yourself of your identity in Christ … make sure you are in honest accountability relationship … avail yourself of the means of grace … wage spiritual warfare against the predator of your soul … get busy serving others with the gifts the Lord has given you … Remember that you accepted by God as his child … ask the Lord to give you his Holy Spirit that you might walk in his ways … set your hope fully on the grace

to be revealed at the revelation of Jesus Christ.[251]

Remembering these important Bible truths will bring peace and victory.

The US military has worked hard toward helping the PTSD service member overcome challenges derived from fighting their country's wars. The religious and secular communities have come to the aid of the soldier in many commendable ways. However, the results of these great efforts have left many healthcare professionals frustrated in not having the results they have hoped for and not being able to solve the problems of PTSD in any significant way. Many patients and health care givers are still committing suicide. Many are still homeless or chronically unemployed while others are still addicted to the medications they thought would help free them from the health issues they face. However, unfortunately, the focus has been laid upon relieving symptoms of problems and not root issues. Drug abuse statistics continue to be staggering.

In serving the service member through spiritual means and attacking root causes of addictions and trauma, I saw first-hand as a chaplain during war the need, and will next describe the method to be promoted for the spiritual survival of the PTSD sufferer through a study in the Word of God. Despite the plethora of self-help support systems and activities available to the soldier with PTSD, including recreational, family, athletic, and health-related help, the problem remains. The critical element that has been left out is spiritual

---

251 David Powlison, *How Does Sanctification Work?* (Wheaton: Crossway, 2017), 288–305 Kindle.

ministering through the soul (mind, will, and emotions) of man. All other efforts may help the individual do better for a time in this life, but the eternal soul and its eternal destination must become an addressed goal. What happens to the soul for all eternity?

Most important are the eternal dividends that are available to those who experience the new birth in Jesus Christ and the hope He gives for eternity as they trust in Him. With all this in view, the methodology is focused upon a relationship with God and placing the hurting warrior in a condition where new life in Christ will be their purpose here in this life and forever in heaven where he/she will have a new mind and a new whole and perfect glorified body forever with God. Consider also the grace that the apostle Paul found through experience in 2 Corinthians 12:9 saying, "My grace is sufficient for thee."

Rich Thomson delivers the biblical approach to counseling apart from humanist psychology in this way: "The Word of God is sufficient and unequalled for counsel concerning man's inner person, because true happiness comes from ordering one's life not according to the counsel of the unbeliever *but* [italics in original] according to Scripture."[252] As he backs his statement with Psalm 1:1–2, Thomson further adds, "… because the believer is warned against embracing any philosophy of living that is not according to Christ."[253] Thomson uses: "See to it that no one takes you captive through philosophy and empty deception, according to the tradition of men, according to the elementary

---
252 Thomson, 7.
253 Ibid., 11.

principles of the world, rather than according to Christ" (Col. 2:8 NASB). Thomson continues, "Because man, in his own wisdom and apart from God's revelation, is not capable of adequately understanding or guiding his inner being."[254] The Bible states in Jeremiah 17:9, "that the heart is deceitful above all things, and desperately wicked." In other texts, Thomson makes clear that the Bible refutes the combining of Scripture with human reasoning. Isaiah uses such verses as: "Thou wilt keep him in perfect peace, whose mind is stayed on thee: because he trusteth in thee" (Isa. 26:3); and "For thus saith the high and lofty One that inhabiteth eternity, whose name is Holy; I dwell in the high and holy place, with him also that is of a contrite and humble spirit, to revive the spirit of the humble, and to revive the heart of the contrite ones" (Isa. 57:15).

The numerous topics and issues involved in PTSD and the various ways those in the medical, psychological, and theological communities respond have been explored. Approaches are wide and varying, and can be overwhelming to those who are already engulfed in the stresses of trauma. Trauma treatment has a long and storied history and has seen a plethora of ways in which the hurting seek relief. The topics for this study are not exhausted, in fact, the DSM volumes continue to be published as man explores more and different types of traumas, disorders, and syndromes to diagnose those who are finding increasingly different ways to be traumatized.

God's love for man is never failing as was demonstrated on the cross of Calvary. Salvation starts

---
254 Ibid., 15.

with the removal of the sin debt and relief of guilt and fear and all things that plague mankind. God can "show himself strong in the behalf of them whose heart is perfect toward him" (2 Chr. 16:9b). Faith in God is the beginning of wisdom as the Proverb proclaims in 1:7. The secular methods of assistance steer away from God and how He is able to make all things new. Adams, through his nouthetic style, points out: "A firm dependence upon the sovereignty of God is a dynamic concept in counseling—one that makes a difference, *the* difference—and, therefore, one that must undergird every effort at counseling."[255] The methodology will be where all ideas are to put into practice and those principles that the Bible teaches help those with PTSD issues to find relief.

Thomson offers this hope to those who suffer:

> The point is abundantly clear in Scripture. If man's inner spirit can endure his physical infirmity—and it can (Prov. 18:14)—and if God will not allow the believer to be tempted beyond what he is able in Christ to endure—and he will not (1 Cor. 10:13)—then the believers material body and brain cannot compel his immaterial heart to entertain or to communicate wrong thoughts, words or actions, nor can his brain and body generate within him the unique heart consequences which issue from those sins: a sense of guilt, apparently uncaused fear, and a desire to flee when there is little or no reason to do so.[256]

---

255 Jay E. Adams, *What About Nouthetic Counseling* (Nutley, NJ: Presbyterian and Reformed Pub, 1976), 11.
256 Thomson, 696–697.

# Epilogue

This book was inspired by the events that occurred to me in 2008 when I was diagnosed with an aortic stenosis (aortic heart valve failure). I was slowly suffocating. After open heart surgery, the Army fixed me up and I was in rehabilitation in the Warrior Transition Battalion with other soldiers rehabbing from surgeries and PTSD. After hearing of soldiers' needs and frustration, these stories stayed with me. I later wrote my doctor of ministry project on the PTSD issues while recovering from colon cancer, chemotherapy, and going through weeks of COVID-19. My prayer is that these collections of thoughts would bring about answers and solve problems, and that those who do not know Jesus Christ personally as Savior would come to know him and to begin their healing process from PTSD.

# Appendix

## Biblical Meditation

Meditation is not memorization. Memorization is not in the Bible. Meditation is—numerous times. "To meditate in it, to read it by day, and think upon it by night. He takes a text and carries it with him all day long, and in the night watches, when sleep forsakes his eyelids he museth upon the Word of God."[257]

Kingsbury explains in his work, *The Benefits and Blessing of Biblical Meditation:*

> Biblical meditation is continually thinking about a specific verse, principle, or truth from the Word of God. It is reminding ourselves and bringing back to our attention something that we know. Here's how it works. In the morning, you read a passage from the Word of God. The Holy Spirit speaks to you in a special way about a certain truth. It sticks with you throughout the day. You repeat the verse over and over.

---

257 Charles Spurgeon, *The Treasury of David* Vol I (Peabody, MA: Hendrickson Pub nd).

> You think about what it means, and how it applies to your life. You consider ways in which you should respond—something particular you should start doing or stop doing or do more of ... and then you do it. When you go to bed at night, that truth is still in your mind.[258]

The Bible's power will manifest itself in what the mind needs at the time as the Word is applied.

Meditation is a crucial element to having proper spiritual ammunition at that moment when the spiritual warfare begins as satanic attacks occur. Again, meditation is not memorization. The spiritual battle will occur in the mind and not in the brain, for this where Satan wages the battle. "For the weapons of our warfare are not carnal (of the body, but mighty through God to the pulling down of strongholds; casting down imaginations, and every high thing that exalteth itself against the knowledge of God, and bringing into captivity every thought to the obedience of Christ" (2 Cor. 10:5). "Be not conformed to this world, but be ye transformed by the renewing of your mind" (Rom. 12:2). See also Isaiah 26:3 and Philippians 4:6–8. Memorization is a brain function; meditation is a heart-and-mind function. Having your guard up at the proper positions at the point of attack is crucial to victory. "But the natural man receiveth not the things of the Spirit of God: for they are foolishness unto him: neither can he know them for they are spitiual discerned. For who hath known the mind of the Lord,

---

258 Kingsbury, *Biblical Meditation*, 42.

that he may instruct him? But we have the mind of Christ" (1 Cor. 2:14, 16).

Another thing to note, according to Kingsbury's *Bblical Meditations,* is that what you think on is a choice. Kingsbury says that you do not have to follow the suggestions from *Biblical Meditations* if you want the same old problems. Meditations are not a once-and-done exercise; it is a daily exercise. The spiritual exercise of Bible meditation is to be considered just as important as breathing. Now, just as there are things recommended for healthy living, there are some things that ought to be eliminated from your thought life, or there will not be a clear line in your thought life toward God. Meditation can get clouded by what you watch, listen to, and read. Conflicts must be resolved in your thought life. *Biblical Meditations* will explain how to have victory in your thought life.

# Glossary

**Adaptive disclosure.** Skills and resources combat veterans need for a lifelong process of forgiveness and hopefulness.

**Behavior health.** Mental health ways of promoting wellbeing and preventing mental illness.

**Budokon.** a yoga, martial arts, and meditation combination.

**Combat fatigue.** World War II term for psychological disturbance caused by exposure to warfare.

**Comorbidity.** The simultaneous presence of two or more chronic diseases or conditions.

**Disarticulation.** The separation of two bones at their joint.

**Dissociation.** A mental escape from distressing experiences during the event.

**Epinephrine.** Adrenaline. The chemical that is released into the body to bring about the ability to react to excitable situations where added strength is required.

**Fugue.** A form of amnesia that involves travel without awareness of how it happens.

**Heimveh.** German term for homesickness, one phrase used to describe PTSD in past wars.

**Humanist.** A way of life that centers on human dignity and worth, rejecting supernaturalism.

**Hyperbaric chamber.** A type of therapy for those who are healing from wounds, thought to assist in curing head trauma from traumatic brain injury.

**Hypervigilance.** The state of being in a continually aroused state of mind. A symptom of PTSD that will not allow an individual to relax and be at rest.

**Lethargy.** A symptom of PTSD. A lack of energy or enthusiasm.

**Maladie du pays.** French term for homesickness.

**Moral injury.** Injury to an individual's moral conscience resulting from an act of perceived moral transgression, producing profound emotional shame.

**Nostalgia.** A sentimental longing for the past, wishing for a time and place of peace (like home—called homesickness). A term used for those who in past wars had PTSD.

**Pharmaceutical.** Drugs that are commercially legal.

**Pluralism.** Ability to cooperate and work with varying faith groups.

**Polypharmacy.** The use of two or more drugs together.

**Recidivism.** A tendency to relapse into a previous condition.

**Resiliency.** The ability to bounce back from adversity.

**Shell shock.** A term used for PTSD during World War I.

**Trigger.** An event, sound, smell, taste, or other sense that reminds one of a past event.

# Selected Bibliography

Adams, Jay E. *Coping With Counseling Crises.* Nutley, NJ: Presbyterian and Reformed Publishing Co., 1977.

———. *How to Help People Change.* Grand Rapids: Zondervan, 1986.

———. *The Chrisitan Counselor's Manual.* Phillipsburg: Presbyterian and Reformed Publishing Co, 1973.

———. *What About Nouthetic Counseling?* Phillipsburg: Presbyterian and Reformed Publishing Co., 1976.

Adsit, Chris. *The Combat Trauma Healing Manual.* Newport News: Military Ministry Press, 2007.

———. *When War Comes Home.* Newport News: Military Ministry Press, 2008.

Ahmad, Ismail Sheikh. *Doing Qualitative Research for Beginners.* Singapore: Partridge Publishing, 2017.

Allender, Dan B. and Tremper Longman III. *The Cry of the Soul.* Colorado Springs: Navpress, 1994.

Anderson, Neil T. *Victory Over the Darkness* Ventura, CA: Regal, 1990.

———. Terry Zuehlke and Julianne S. Zuehlke. *Christ Centered Therapy,* Grand Rapids: Zondervan, 2000.

Arterburn, Stephen and Jack Felton. *Toxic Faith: Experiencing Healing from Painful Spiritual Abuse.* Colorado Springs, CO; Waterbrook Press, 2001.

Bannerman, Stacy. *When the War Came Home.* New York: Continuum, 2006.

Barrett, Lisa Feldman. *How Emotions Are Made.* New York: Houghton, Mifflin, Harcourt, 2017.

Beattie, Melody. *Codependent No More.* Center City, MN: Hazeldon, 1987.

Benimoff, Roger. *Faith Under Fire.* New York: Crown Publishers, 2009.

Benner, David G. *Care of Souls.* Grand Rapids: Baker, 1998.

Berg, Jim *Taking Time to Quiet Your Soul.* Greenville, SC: JourneyForth Books, 2005.

Bilton, Michael and Kevin Sim. *Four Hours in My Lai.* New York: Penguin, 1992.

Boice, James Montgomery. *Renewing Your Mind in a Mindless World.* Grand Rapids: Kregel, 1993.

Bobgan, Martin and Deidre. *Against Biblical Counseling, For the Bible.* Santa Barbara, CA: EastGate, 1994.

———. *Christ-Centered Ministry Versus Problem-Solving Counseling.* Santa Barbara: EastGate, 2004.

———. *Competent to Minister.* Santa Barbara: EastGate, 1996.

———. *Hypnosis: Medical, Scientific or Occultic.* Santa Barbara: EastGate, 2001.

———. *Person to Person Ministry.* Santa Barbara: EastGate, 2009.

———. *Prophets of PsychoHeresy I.* Santa Barbara: EastGate, 1988.

———. *Prophets of PsychoHeresy II.* Santa Barbara: EastGate, 1990.

———. *PsychoHeresy.* Santa Barbara: EastGate, 2012.

———. *The End of Christian Psychology.* Santa Barbara: EastGate, 1997.

Bounds, E.M. *The Complete Works of E.M. Bounds on Prayer.* Grand Rapids: Baker Books, 1990.

Brand, Paul and Philip Yancey. *Pain, The Gift Nobody Wants.* New York: Harper Collins, 1993.

Burks, Benjamin R. and George T. Crabb. *Codependency.* Rockford, IL: Reformers Unanimous, 2012.

Campbell, Duncan. *The Power and Price of Revival.* Rockford, IL: Reformers Unanimous, nd.

Cantrell, Bridget C. and Chuck Dean. *Down Range: To Iraq and Back.* Seattle: Wordsmith Books, 2005.

Carlisle, Rodney P. General Ed. *Handbook to Life in America: The Gilded Age.* New York: Infobase Pub, 2009.

Carragher, Douglas J. *Wounded Spirits: A Biblical Approach to Dealing with the Effects of Post Traumatic Stress Disorder.* Second Edition. Murfreesboro, TN: Walden Way, 2017.

Cervantes, Cisco. *Self-Destruct: Break the Cycle of Self-Damaging Behavior.* Rockford, IL: Reformers Unanimous, 2018.

Chadwick, Samuel. *The Way to Pentecost.* Rockford, Il: Reformers Unanimous, nd.

Chapman, Gary. *The Five Love Languages.* Chicago: Northfield, 1992.

Clark Allen. *Wounded Soldier, Healing Warrior.* St Paul: Zenith Press, 2007.

Cline, Lydia S. *Today's Military Wife.* Mechanicsburg, PA: Stackpole Books, 1998.

Cole, Darrell. *When God Says War Is Right.* Colorado Springs: Waterbrook Press, 2002.

Collins, Gary R. *Christian Counseling.* Nashville: Thomas Nelson, 2007.

―――. *The Biblical Basis of Christian Counseling for People Helpers.* Colorado Springs: Navpress, 2001.

Copan, Paul. *True For You, But Not For Me.* Minneapolis: Bethany, 1998.

―――. and Scott B. Luley and Stanley W. Wallace, ed. *Philosophy: Christian Perspective for the New Millenium.* Addison, TX., Norcross, GA. CLM and RZIM, 2003.

Crabb. George T., *Anger,* Rockford, IL: Reformers Unanimous, 2010.

―――. *Diagnostic and Spiritual Manual, Vol 1.* Rockford, IL: Reformers Unanimous, 2011.

―――. *Diagnostic and Spiritual Manual, Vol 2.* Rockford, IL: Reformers Unanimous, 2012.

―――. *Just Say No.* Rockford, IL: Steven Boyd Pub, 2007.

———. *The Scorn of Porn*. Rockford, IL: Reformers Unanimous, 2009.

Crabb, George T. and Benjamin R. Burks. *Battle for the Soul*. Rockford, IL: Reformers Unanimous, 2014.

———. and Benjamin R. Burks. *Recovery Without Relapse*. Rockford, IL: Reformers Unanimous, 2009.

Creswell, John W. *Research Design: Qualitative, Quantitative, and Mixed Method Approaches*. Thousand Oaks, CA: Sage. 2003.

Curington, Steven B. *Discover of Recovery*. Rockford, IL: Steven Boyd Pub, 2010.

———. *Nevertheless I Live*. Rockford, IL: Steven Boyd Pub, 2004.

———. *Preparing for Peace*. Rockford, IL: Steven Boyd Pub, 2009.

———. *Produce the Juice*. Rockford, IL: Steven Boyd Pub, 2006.

———. *Tall Law*. Rockford, IL: Steven Boyd Pub., 2005.

———. *Umbrella Fella*. Rockford, IL: Steven Boyd Pub, 2007.

Darmofal, Kelly Bouldin. *Lost in My Mind*. Ann Arbor, MI: Modern History Press, 2014.

Dean, Chuck and Bette Nordberg. *When the War Is Over a New One Begins*. Seattle: Word Smith Publishing, 2003.

Denton, Jeremiah A. Jr. *When Hell Was in Session*. Washington, DC: Morley Books, 1997.

Dewey, Larry. *War and Redemption.* Burlington, VT: Ashgate Publishing Co., 2004.

Dobson, Edward G. *Annotated Study Bible.* Nashville, TN: Thomas Nelson, 1975.

Dobson, James. *What Wives Wish Their Husbands Knew about Women.* Wheaton: Tyndale House, 1975.

———. *When God Doesn't Make Sense.* Wheaton: Tyndale House, 1993.

Dodes, Lance and Zachary Dodes. *The Sober Truth.* Boston: Beacon Press, 2014.

Dunn, James D. G. *Word Biblical Commentary Romans 1–8.* Dallas: Word, 1988.

Egendorf, Arthur. *Healing From the War.* Boston: Houghton Mifflin, 1985.

Ehrenwald, Jan. *The History of Psychotherapy.* Northvale, NJ: Jason Aronson Inc., 1991.

Feldman, Lisa Barrett. *How Emotions Are Made.* New York: Houghton Mifflin Harcourt, 2017.

F.C. Cook Ed. *The Bible Commentary Vol IX Romans to Philemon.* Grand Rapids: Baker, 1981.

Figley, Charles B. and William P. Nash. *Combat Stress Injury.* New York: Routledge, 2007.

Finney, Charles G. *Power From on High. Rockford, Il: Reformers Unanimous, nd.*

Frankl, Viktor E. *Man's Search for Meaning.* Boston: Beacon Press, 1959.

Fuller, Robert C. *Americans and the Unconscious.* New York: Oxford Press, 1986.

Gaebelein, Frank E. "Genesis." In *Genesis.* Vol. II of *Expositors Bible Commentary.* Grand Rapids: Zondervan, 1979.

Gilley, Gary. *This Little Church Went to Market.* Webster, NY: Evangelical Press, 2005.

Gould, Joe. *Army Recognizes Humanism as a Religious Preference.* Army Times, May 5, 2014.

Griggs, Robert W. *A Pelican of the Wilderness.* Eugene, OR: Cascade, 2014.

Griffin, Jay and Ryan Jiles. *God's Plan for Rebuilding and Restoration.* Rockford, IL: Reformers Unanimous, 2014.

Grimsley, Charles W. *PTSD and Moral Injury.* Maitland, FL; Xulon Press, 2017.

Grogan, Geoffrey W., "Isaiah." In *Isaiah-Ezekiel,* Vol. 6 of *The Expositor's Bible Commentary,* edited by Frank E. Gaebelein. Grand Rapids: Zondervan, 1986.

Grossman, Dave. *On Killing.* Boston: Backbay Books., 1996.

Guiness, Os. *Unspeakable: Facing up to Evil in an Age of Genocide and Terror.* San Francisco: Harper, 2005.

Gwynn, J. "Philippians." In *Romans to Philemon.* Vol IX of *The Bible Commentary,* edited by F.C. Cook. Grand Rapids: Baker Books, 1981.

Habermas, Gary R. *Why Is God Ignoring Me.* Carol Stream, IL: Tyndale, 2010.

Hadley, Donald W. and Gerald T. Richards. *Ministry with the Military.* Grand Rapids: Baker, 1992.

Hessamfar, Elahe. *In the Fellowship of His Suffering: A Theological Interpretation of Mental Illness.* Eugene, OR: Cascade Books, 2014.

Hicks, Robert. *Failure to Scream.* Nashville: Thomas Nelson, 1993.

———. *Returning Home.* Tarrytown: Fleming H. Revell, 1973.

———. *Trauma: The Pain That Stays.* Grand Rapids: Fleming H. Revell, 1993.

Hunt, Dave. *Occult Invasion.* Eugene, OR: Harvest House, 1998.

———. *Yoga and the Body of Christ.* Bend, OR: Berean Call, 2006.

Hutchins, James M. *Beyond Combat.* Great Falls, MN: Shepherd Press. 1968.

Hux, Karens. *Assisting Survivors of TBI.* Austin, TX: Pro-Ed, 2003.

Jamieson, Faucette. Brown. *A Commentary: Critical, Experimental and Practical Vol II.* Grand Rapids: Eerdman, 1978.

Janosik, Ellen. *Crisis Counseling.* Boston: Jones-Bartlett Pub., 1994.

Jiles, Ryan and Benjamin Burks. *Seasons of Addiction.* Loves Park, IL: RU Pub, 2016.

Jones, William, J.W. Burn, George Barbol. *The Preachers Complete Homeletic Commentary.* Grand Rapids: Baker, nd.

Jones, Serene. *Trauma and Grace.* Louisville, KY: Westminster John Knox Press, 2009.

Kay, Ellie. *Heroes at Home.* Bloomington, IL: Bethany House, 2002.

Kingsbury, Paul. *Adversity University.* Rockford, IL: Reformers Unanimous, 2011.

———. *Rescue and Recover.* Rockford, IL: Reformers Unanimous, 2011.

———. *The Benefits and Blessings of Biblical Meditation.* Loves Park, IL: Reformers Unanimous, 2018.

Kubler-Ross, Elizabeth. *On Death and Dying.* New York: McMillian Publishing, 1969.

Kuenning, Delores. *Helping People Through Grief.* Minneapolis: Bethany House, 1987.

Lambert, Heath. *A Theology of Biblical Counseling.* Grand Rapids: Zondervan, 2016.

———. *The Gospel and Mental Health.* Middletown, DE: Association of Certified Biblical Counselors, 2014.

Leyva, Meredith. *Married to the Military.* New York: Simon and Schuster, 2003.

MacArthur, Jr., John F. and Wayne Mack. *Introduction to Biblical Counseling.* Dallas: Word Pub, 1994.

Mack, Wayne A. *Anger and Stress.* Phillipsburg, PA: Calvary Press, 2004. Kindle.

Makari, George. *Revolution in Mind.* New York: Harper Collins, 2008.

Mansfield, Stephen. *The Faith of the American Soldier.* New York: Penguin, 2005.

Marshall, S. L. A. *The Problem of Batle Command in Future War.* New York: William Morrow and Company, 1947.

Martin, Hillary. *Solo-Ops: A Survival Guide for Military Wives.* Broomfield, CO: Xlibris Corp, 2003.

Matsakis, Aphrodite. *Back from the Front.* Baltimore: Sidron Inst Press, 2007.

———. *I Can't Get Over It: The Handbook for Trauma Survivors.* Oakland, CA: New Harbinger Publishing, 1992.

Maynard, Kyle. *No Excuses.* Washington, DC: Regnery, 2005.

Menniger, Karl. *Whatever Became of Sin?* New York, NY: Hawthorne Books, 1973.

McConkey, James H. *The Three-Fold Secret of the Holy Spirit.* Rockford, IL: Reformers Unanimous, nd.

Meager, Robert Emmet. *Killing From the Inside Out: Moral Injury and Just War.* Eugene, OR: Cascade Books, 2014.

Meyer, F. B. *The Secret of Guidance.* Rockford, IL: Reformers Unanimous, nd.

———. *The Way into the Holiest.* Rockford, IL: Reformers Unanimous, nd.

Moody, D. L. *Prevailing Prayer.* Greenville: Ambassador, 1997.

Morgan, G. Campbell. *The Practice of Prayer.* Greenville: Ambassador, 1925.

Mueller, George. *Answers to Prayer.* Chicago: Moody Press, nd.

Murphy, Audie. *To Hell and Back.* New York: Holt, 1949.

Murray, Andrew. *Absolute Surrender.* Rockford, IL: Reformers Unanimous, nd.

———. *The Deeper Christian Life.* Rockford, IL: Reformers Unanimous, nd.

Myers, David G, Jones, Stanton L., Roberts Robert C., Watson, Paul J., Coe, John H., Hall, Todd W., Powlison, David, *Psychology and Christianity. Five Views,* Edited by Eric L. Johnson, Downers Grover, IL: IVP Academic, 2010.

Newport, John. *The New Age Movement and the Biblical Worldview.* Grand Rapids: Eerdmans, 1998.

Oakland, Roger. *Faith Undone,* Silverton, OR: Lighthouse Trails Publishing, 2007.

Pavlicin, Karen M. *Surviving Deployment.* Saint Paul: Elva Resa Publishing, 2003.

Peele, Stanton. *Diseasing of America: Addiction Treatment out of Control.* Lexington, MA: Lexington Books, 1989.

Phillips, John. *Exploring Romans: Expositors Commentary.* Grand Rapids: Kregel, 1969.

Pitts, Charles F. *Chaplains in Gray.* Nashville, TN: Broadman, 1957.

Powlison, David. *How Does Sanctification Work?* Wheaton: Crossway, 2017. Kindle.

Pryde, Debi. *Why Am I So Angry?* Newberry Springs, CA: Iron Sharpeneth Iron Pub, nd.

Raddatz, Martha. *The Long Road Home.* New York: Penguin, 2007.

Redmond, Jessica. *A Year of Absence.* St Paul: Elva Resa, 2005.

Rickenbacher, Edward V. *Seven Came Through.* Garden City, NY: Doubleday. 1943.

Sanders, Catherine M. *Grief, The Morning After.* New York: John Wiley and Sons, 1999.

Schnurr, Paula P. "Finding Social Benefit After a Collective Trauma." *Journal of Traumatic Stress,* 44, no.2 (April 2009): 81.

Scholten, Robert. *Psalm Twenty-Five & PTSD.* Mustang, OK: Tate Publishing, 2011.

Shay, Jonathan. *Achilles in Vietnam.* New York: Scribner, 1994.

———. *Odysseus in America.* New York: Scribner, 2002.

Sincair, N. Duncan. *Horrific Traumata.* New York: Hawthorne Press, 1993.

Spurgeon, Charles H. *Treasury of David.* Grand Rapids: Kregel, 1976.

Stanley, Charles. *The Gift of Forgiveness.* Nashville: Thomas Nelson, 1981.

Szasz, Thomas. *Psychiatry: The Science of Lies.* Syracuse, NY: Syracuse University Press, 2008.

———. *The Myth of Psychotherapy.* Syracuse, NY: Syracuse Press, 1988.

Tenney, Merrill C. *The Zondervan Encyclopedia of the Bible.* Grand Rapids: Zondervan, 2009.

Thomson, Rich. *The Heart of Man and the Mental Disorders.* Alief, TX: Biblical Counseling Ministries, Inc., 2012.

Tick Edward. *War of the Soul.* Wheaton: Quest Books, 2005.

———. *Warrior's Return, Restoring the Soul After War.* Boulder, CO: Sounds True, 2014.

Torrey, R. A. *How to Pray.* Rockford, Il: Reformers Unanimous, nd.

Turabian, Kate L. *A Manual for Writers.* 8th ed. Chicago: University of Chicago, 2013.

Tyson, Ann Scott. *American Spartan.* New York: Harper Collins, 2014.

Vandergriff, Don. *The Path to Victory.* Kabul, Afghanistan: Don Vandergriff, 2013.

Vandesteeg, Carol. *When Duty Calls.* Enumclaw, WA: Winepress Publishing, 2001

Veith Jr, Gene Edward. *Postmodern Times: A Christian Guide to Contemporary Thought and Culture.* Wheaton: Crossway Books, 1994.

Vyhmeister, Nancy Jean. *Quality Research Papers.* Grand Rapids: Zondervan, 2008.

Walzer, Michael. *Just and Unjust Wars.* New York: Basic Books, 1977.

Weber, Stu. *Spirit Warrior.* Sister, OR: Multnomah Publishers, 2001

Webster, Alexander F.C. and Darrell Cole. *The Virtue of War.* Salisbury, MA: Regina Orthodox Press, 2004.

Webster, Noah. *American Dictionary of the English Language.* San Francisco: Foundation for American Christian Education, 1967.

Williams, Mary Beth and Soili Poijiule. *The PTSD Workbook.* Oakland, CA: New Harbinger, 2002.

Wood, David. *What Have We Done.* New York: Little Brown, 2016.

Wright, H. Norman. *Crisis and Trauma Counseling.* Ventura: Regal Books, 2003.

Wurmbrand, Richard. *Reaching Toward the Heights.* Bartlesville, OK: Living Sacrifice Book Co, 1979.

———. *Tortured for Christ.* Middlebury, VT: Living Sacrifice Books, 1985.

Zacharias, Ravi. *Beyond Opinion: Living the Faith We Defend.* Nashville: Thomas Nelson, 2007.

# PERIODICALS

Rauch, Angelica. *Post Traumatic Hermeneutic: Melancholia in Wake of Trauma.* Vol. 28 no. 4 (Winter 1998).

# Electronic Documents

After Deployment. "A Mental Wellness Resource for Service Members, Veterans and their Families." http://www.afterdeployment.org (accessed March 21, 2009).

A Primer for Employers, www.workplacementalhealth.org. Accessed 11 Apr. 2020.

Bare, Stacy. *Truth About 22 Veterans Suicides a Day.* 20 July, 2017. www.taskandpurpose.com.

Brain Trauma Foundation. *Predictive Brain State.* http://www.braintrauma.org (accessed January, 2009).

Department of Veterans Affairs. "National Center for Post-Traumatic Stress Disorder." http://www.ncptsd.va.gov (accessed March 26, 2009).

Leys, Ruth. *Trauma Cures, Shell Shock, Janet and the Questions of Memory.* Vol 20, no.4, (Summer 1994), 111–120. Accessed June 9, 2017.

Life Model. "Trauma and Recovery." http://www.lifemodel.org (accessed January, 2009).

McMahon, T.A. 2018. "The Avatar—A Newsletter Classic." The Berean Call, June. Accessed June 9, 2018. http://www.thebereancall.com.

Revelant, Julie, "How Trauma in the Military Can Lead to PTSD and How to Find Relief for You and Your Loved Ones" www.EverydayHealth.com, 20 April, 2018.

Stahl, Ronit Y. *Atheists in Foxholes*. Religion and Politics, Oct 21, 2014.

US War Department. *Night Combat*. D.A. Pamphlet 2–256, Jun 1953.

http://www.frc.org (accessed date 20 May, 2019).

http://www.menslegal.com. (Accessed 12 May, 2020).

http://www.ncbi.nim.mih.gov/pmc, 2 Nov, 2018. (Accessed 11 Apr 2020).

http://www.ptsd.va.gov/public/treatment-med/mindfulness-ptsd.ssp.

http://www.rtmtraingcenter.com, (Accessed 11 Apr 2020).

http://www.military.com, Sisk, Richard 8 July 2017.

http://www.taskandpurpose.com. (Access date 12 Dec 2017).

http://www.warriortraining.us. (Access date 21 Jan. 2018).

http://www.workplacementalhealth.org. 12 May, 2020.

Milton Keynes UK
Ingram Content Group UK Ltd.
UKHW021445011224
451693UK00013B/1178

9 798893 895277